DYNAMICS OF FAITH

paul tillich

DYNAMICS
OF FAITH

PERENNIAL ■ CLASSICS

A hardcover edition of this book was originally published in 1957 by Harper & Row, Publishers. It was originally Volume X of the World Perspectives series edited by Ruth Nanda Anshen.

HarperCollins books may be purchased for educational, business, or sales promotional use. For information please write: Special Markets Department, HarperCollins Publishers Inc., 10 East 53rd Street, New York, NY 10022.

First Harper paperback edition published 1958.
First Perennial Classics edition published 2001.
Perennial Classics are published by Perennial, an imprint of Harper-Collins Publishers.

Library of Congress Cataloging-in-Publication Data

Tillich, Paul, 1886–1965.
    Dynamics of faith / Paul Tillich. — 1st Perennial classics ed.
        p.   cm. — (Perennial classics)
    Originally published: New York : Harper, © 1957, in series: World perspectives.
    ISBN 0-06-093713-0
    1. Faith.   I. Title.   II. Perennial classic.

    BT771.2.T54   2001
    234'.23—dc21   2001024816

        04 05 FG/RRD 10 9 8

CONTENTS

🞨 Contents

INTRODUCTION TO
THE PERENNIAL CLASSICS EDITION

Paul Tillich was one of the great Protestant philoso-
pher/theologians of the twentieth century. His long
and extraordinary career took root in his native Germany and flourished in the United States, especially
during the last ten years of his life. During that time
hundreds of students filled his classes; hundreds
and sometimes thousands, both young and old,
attended his public lectures and sermons. He was a
prolific author, and his books were widely read. The
more popular ones, such as *The Courage to Be* and
Dynamics of Faith, became bestsellers. His *Collected
Works* comprise fourteen volumes, not including the
magisterial three-volume *Systematic Theology* (his
magnum opus) or his three volumes of sermons. It
is not surprising, therefore, that Reinhold Niebuhr,
who dominated the American theological scene
until the mid-1950s, described his friend and colleague as "a seminal theologian."

Tillich's enormous success toward the end of his
life did not surprise his colleagues and friends, for he

was a mesmerizing master teacher and a charismatic preacher. It *is* remarkable, however, that his influence became deeper and wider in the last phases of his career, when the opposite might have been expected. His books were read by countless ministers, laypersons, and students across all denominations in American Protestantism, and his work engaged the attention of many who had little or no relationship with either the Christian churches or with organized religion.

Tillich, moreover, was a deeply loyal man who remained faithful to his own calling. At an early age he was drawn to theology and philosophy, and cast aside earlier dreams of becoming an architect. He was a humanist in the fullest sense of the word: he was filled with a high personal sense of the character of civilization. He remembered important lessons he learned from his teachers and friends. Wilhelm Pauck, the historical theologian who was his close friend and colleague, referred to him as "an autobiographical thinker."

Paul Johannes Oskar Tillich was born in 1886 in a tiny village in Prussia, Germany, where his father was a high official in the Evangelical Prussian Lutheran Church. His early youth was steeped in nineteenth-century optimism, encouraged by the sound of military marching bands and made secure by a feudalistic monarchy. Until his fourteenth year, he lived in a small medieval town in Brandenburg in the middle of Prussia. Gothic churches and old houses gave him a feeling of continuity. Later on, he lived in Berlin, which ignited his passion for big cities. As a child, Tillich lived a life of "dreaming innocence." He played with his younger sisters in a garden surrounded by high walls. He was a "little bit in love" with his mother, who died when he was seventeen. In some ways he sought to replace her ever after. He also loved his father, but he was in awe of him. In discussions with his father at an early age, Tillich wondered aloud about the idea of "nothingness," i.e. the Greek philosopher Parmenides' question, "Why is there not nothing?" For the young Tillich, his father's authority was both personal and intellectual; it was, therefore, difficult for him to question his father's orthodox views about Christian thought without feeling guilty.

As it happened, when he attended the universities in Halle and Tübingen, Tillich was given the chance to question authority as often as he wished. At Halle he was influenced by the systematic theologian Martin Kähler, who combined a sympathetic understanding of the faith of the Protestant reformers, especially Luther, with an openness to the humanism of the German literary classics, especially Goethe. Tillich was indebted to Kähler for a constructive understanding of the doctrine of justifica-

tion by faith. Moreover, he found himself stimulated
to apply its meaning also to the realm of intellectual
thought. This means that we are justified by becoming acceptable in God's sight even though we are
sinners but also when we are doubters. Tillich,
therefore, never became dogmatic. Kähler intro-
duced the idea of mediation to Tillich, who in later
years wrote an autobiographical essay titled "On the
Boundary," describing his existence as between philosophy and theology, between human culture and
religion, and between the secular and the sacred.
Kähler also suggested to Tillich that the Christian
faith is not centered in the Jesus of history, but in
Jesus *as he is believed to be the Christ*, i.e. the Messiah
and Redeemer.

While in Halle, Tillich also studied with Fritz
Medicus, a docent of philosophy who later occupied
the philosophical chair at the Zurich Institute of
Technology. He suggested that Tillich write a dis-
sertation on the works of Schelling. Tillich absorbed
Schelling to such an extent that the latter's ideas
became part and parcel of his own work, especially
the conception of themes like the *Kairos* (the right
time) and the demonic. Tillich remained faithful to
Kähler and Medicus throughout his life.

Tillich was a member of a famous corporation
of students: the Christian student fraternity known
as "Wingolf." He was the first officer of its chapter

at the university, and he presided over many lively discussions about the principles that were to guide students in their common life. He recalled those times in a famous letter written to Thomas Mann (23 May 1943): "What I have become as a philosopher, a man, I owe partly to my professors but mostly to this fraternity. The theological and philosophical debates we had then till late after midnight and the personal conversations in which we were engaged before dawn, have remained decisive for my entire life." It should be noted that Tillich's style of discussion and debate was never confrontational; Reinhold Niebuhr called him "a pacific theologian."

＊Shortly after Tillich had finished his doctoral program and had established himself as a pastor in the Evangelical Prussian Lutheran Church, the First World War broke out. He enlisted and became an army chaplain on the German front. Tillich's youth thus came abruptly to an end. He had been steeped in the spirit of the nineteenth century, with its confidence in the human ability to master nature and the difficulties of life. During the war, he experienced the breakdown of the self-assurance of this proud civilization. He always remembered that during a frightful night on the battlefield of Verdun he had seen, as in a vision, the end of the era of monarchies and the end of Protestant bourgeois civilization. On that night, as he fearlessly attempted to drag the wounded away from the line of fire, he experienced despair.

Tillich had married shortly before the war began. When he returned to Berlin in 1919, he discovered that his wife had been unfaithful to him and that she was bearing his best friend's child. In the midst of postwar chaos and personal distress, he plunged into the vital and sympathetic life of the Bohéme in Berlin. He yearned for freedom from the absolute authority he had experienced at home as well as freedom from the suffocating moralism of the Wingolf fraternity. After divorcing his first wife, he married the poetic and artistic Hannah Werner. This marriage lasted until Tillich's death in 1965.

Despite the breakdown of civilization as he had known it, Tillich courageously chose to join other young men of hope who worked to rebuild European culture. In Berlin he belonged to a circle called the Religious Socialists and soon became their most creative thinker and leading spokesman. The group was small and had loyal followers but no political power. Large numbers of Nazis and Communists and splinter parties continued their struggle for power as economic depression and inflation impoverished the German people, and all too soon the brief shining moment known as the Weimar Republic was over. Hitler came to power and the reign of terror began.

Tillich occupied an influential chair in philosophy at the University of Frankfurt when he was dismissed by Hitler's government. One might say that his dismissal was a blessing in disguise. Through the efforts of Reinhold Niebuhr, he was invited to Union Theological Seminary in New York, where he continued to work with the same ideas that had preoccupied him from the beginning of his career. The mere fact that his complex and sometimes obscure thought was accepted in an intellectual climate marked by practicality is astonishing. He painstakingly learned English at the age of forty-seven and mastered the language, if not the pronunciation, often saying that English had clarified his abstract ideas and made them more understandable. Though he did not find it easy to adapt to conditions at Union, he willingly took up new responsibilities. He once said that in Frankfurt he had been a full professor but at Union he had been reduced to a mere docent; yet he never complained, and he never looked back.

As the students and faculty soon found out, Tillich was not a historian but his thought was permeated with the history of mankind, with cultural history, and, especially, with the history of Christian theological and philosophical thought. In his teaching and writing, as well as in private meditations and conversations, Tillich roamed through history trying to bring it to bear on the modern cultural and spiritual crisis—a crisis that he tried to view through the eyes of such diagnosticians as Kierkegaard, Dostoyevsky, Nietzsche, Marx and Freud. He incorporated ideas from Plato and Plotinus (the essences); the Stoics (the Logos); Augustine on grace; Eckhart (God is Being); Cusanus on the coincidence of opposites; and most especially Luther, with his interpretation of the Christian message in terms of justification by faith and his teachings on the God of judgment and mercy, wrath and love; Böhme, with his brooding on God as the ground and abyss of being; and the great German thinkers Kant, Hegel and, most especially, Schelling. The ideas of liberal theologians from Schleiermacher to Troeltsch, who had renounced the supernaturalistic authorities of the past in order to attempt a historical interpretation of the Christian religion, were transformed by Tillich. Like a sponge, he soaked up the major themes of Christian doctrine only to give them new life in his system. In the classroom, students were treated to the first readings of Tillich's systematic theology; many were spellbound as they observed his system building-block by building-block.

Outside the classroom he participated to some extent in American politics during World War II: he joined the Fellowship of Socialist Christians and supported the New Deal. He established Self Help, an organization which found jobs and homes for refugees. He broadcast radio sermons and addresses to the German people urging them to continue their fight against the Nazi rulers. Tillich hoped that after victory over Hitler was achieved there would be a constructive peace settlement—one resulting in an international union of the nations of the world. But these hopes were dashed by Winston Churchill's announcement of the "cold war" and of the "iron curtain" between the East and the West or between the U.S.S.R. and the Western powers, especially the United States. Tillich resignedly proclaimed the doctrine of the "sacred void," a period of waiting for the right moment (*Kairos*) to act.

Tillich and many other German-speaking American professors were invited to lecture in Germany in 1949. He was given a wide and enthusiastic hearing; friends and colleagues had not forgotten Tillich. Indeed, several universities offered him academic positions, but he did not accept them. The several honors eventually showered upon him by the German government, such as the Order of Merit, the Goethe Prize, and the Peace Prize of German Publishers and Booksellers, demonstrate that his frequent appearances in Germany exerted a powerful influence.

During this third phase of the historical period in which Tillich lived, he felt he should help his contemporaries withstand the existential problems and difficulties that tend to emerge in a time of cultural transition. It was clear to him that because traditional values had lost their appeal, many people were overcome by a sense of emptiness. They had become victims of the anxiety of meaninglessness. Accordingly, Tillich tried to understand the human situation as deeply and fully as possible, paying attention not only to special problems in ecclesiastical and political systems but also the structures of human anxiety, conflict, and guilt. Tillich therefore endeavored to interpret the Christian message so that his contemporaries would be able to understand it as a living gospel, one that would speak to *them*. He hoped that a reinterpretation of Christian symbols and forms of expression would renew their power.

Tillich made a supreme effort to carry out this task. He was sometimes called an "apostle to the intellectuals," one who spoke in their language. As Wilhelm Pauck has pointed out, this is only partly true. Although Tillich tried to interpret the Christian religion for intellectuals who had been thrown into spiritual emptiness—a condition caused by secularization—he did not, in fact, speak their language; he understood their condition and empathized with their anxiety, but he spoke to them in *his own* language. Essentially, Tillich feared that modern civilization, having ceased to be theonomous, might fall under demonic control. Indeed, this had already happened for a time under the Nazi and Bolshevik dictatorships and in similar movements and tendencies throughout Western civilization.

In defining religion, which he regarded as "the substance, the ground and the depth of man's spiritual life," Tillich employed the term *ultimate concern*. "Religion," or "faith," he said, is the state of being grasped by the power of "being itself," by an "unconditional concern" or by "that which concerns one unconditionally." This is Tillich's own definition, though it sounds very much like Luther's famous interpretation: "Faith is the state of being grasped by that which concerns one unconditionally."

※ Another interesting concept Tillich used was the *New Being*. Here he was thinking of Paul's saying in 2 Cor. 5:17: "If any man is in Christ, he is a new creature: the old things are passed way; behold, they are become new." This illustrates perfectly Tillich's conviction that the "old symbols," namely doctrines, creedal and liturgical formulas, must be "deliteralized." He did not think that these terms should be demythologized, but he felt that, instead of being interpreted literally, they should be taken spiritually. He expressed their meaning in terms he had derived either from historical tradition or from contemporary experience, speaking of sin as estrangement, of grace as acceptance, of the Holy Spirit as spiritual presence.

 ✳ In his book *The Dynamics of Faith*, which is the best popular introduction to his thought available today, he tells the reader what faith is and what it is not. He describes the symbols of faith, the types of faith, the truth of faith, and finally, the life of faith. He chooses a word in religious language which is subject to more misunderstanding, distortions, and questionable definitions than any other, and what he says about faith is still valid today. It is the confusion about the word "faith" that creates skepticism, Tillich argues. If he were able to find a new word for "faith," he writes, he would do so, but there is no such word. Tillich reinterpreted the word for the readers of his day and in many ways his interpretations are still valid today. He still dares us to give ourselves to something larger than we are in the hope that we shall find our true selves: this "giving ourselves to something larger" is the heart of religious faith.

In explaining the meaning of these terms, Tillich sought to be both a true diagnostician of the human situation as well as a true and radical spokesman of "ultimate concern [i.e., God]." His wonder—that there is *being* and *not nothing*; that there is *meaning* (residing in truth, beauty, and goodness) and not *meaninglessness*; that all beings and meanings are dependent, in terms of origin and destiny, upon being itself—was as powerful in his old age as it was in his youth.

During his lifetime, Tillich attracted enthusiastic audiences and influenced their thinking. He has been dead for almost thirty-six years, and although he did not found a school, his work lives on in the academic, religious, and secular worlds.

Marion Pauck
Palo Alto, California
May 2001

INTRODUCTORY REMARKS

There is hardly a word in the religious language, both theological and popular, which is subject to more misunderstandings, distortions and questionable definitions than the word "faith." It belongs to those terms which need healing before they can be used for the healing of men. Today the term "faith" is more productive of disease than of health. It confuses, misleads, creates alternately skepticism and fanaticism, intellectual resistance and emotional surrender, rejection of genuine religion and subjection to substitutes. Indeed, one is tempted to suggest that the word "faith" should be dropped completely; but desirable as that may be it is hardly possible. A powerful tradition protects it. And there is as yet no substitute expressing the reality to which the term "faith" points. So, for the time being, the only way of dealing with the problem is to try to reinterpret the word and remove the confusing and distorting connotations, some of which are the heritage of centuries. It is the hope of the writer that he will succeed at least in this purpose even if he does not succeed in his more far-reaching aim to convince some readers of the hidden power of faith within themselves and of the infinite significance of that to which faith is related.

Cambridge, September 1956

DYNAMICS OF FAITH

I

⊠

WHAT FAITH IS

1. Faith As Ultimate Concern

Faith is the state of being ultimately concerned: the dynamics of faith are the dynamics of man's ultimate concern. Man, like every living being, is concerned about many things, above all about those which condition his very existence, such as food and shelter. But man, in contrast to other living beings, has spiritual concerns—cognitive, aesthetic, social, political. Some of them are urgent, often extremely urgent, and each of them as well as the vital concerns can claim ultimacy for a human life or the life of a social group. If it claims ultimacy it demands the total surrender of him who accepts this claim, and it promises total fulfillment even if all other claims have to be subjected to it or rejected in its name. If a national group makes the life and growth of the nation its ultimate concern, it demands that all other concerns, economic well-being, health and life, family, aesthetic and cognitive truth, justice and humanity, be sacrificed. The extreme nationalisms of our century are laboratories for the study of what ultimate concern means in all aspects of human existence, including the smallest concern of one's daily life. Everything is centered in the only god, the nation—a god who certainly proves to be a demon, but who shows clearly the unconditional character of an ultimate concern.

But it is not the unconditional demand made by that which is one's ultimate concern, it is also the promise of ultimate fulfillment which is accepted in the act of faith. The content of this promise is not necessarily defined. It can be expressed in indefinite symbols or in concrete symbols which cannot be taken literally, like the "greatness" of one's nation in which one participates even if one has died for it, or the conquest of mankind by the "saving race," etc. In each of these cases it is "ultimate fulfillment" that is promised, and it is exclusion from such fulfillment which is threatened if the unconditional demand is not obeyed.

An example—and more than an example—is the faith manifest in the religion of the Old Testament. It also has the character of ultimate concern in demand, threat and promise. The content of this concern is not the nation—although Jewish nationalism has sometimes tried to distort it into that—but the content is the God of justice, who, because he represents justice for everybody and every nation, is called the universal God, the God of the universe. He is the ultimate concern of every pious Jew, and therefore in his name the great commandment is given: "You shall love the Lord your God with all your heart, and with all your soul, and with all your might" (Deut. 6:5). This is what ultimate concern means and from these words the term "ultimate concern" is derived. They state unambiguously the character of genuine faith, the demand of total surrender to the subject of ultimate concern. The Old Testament is full of commands which make the nature of this surrender concrete, and it is full of promises and threats in relation to it. Here also are the promises of symbolic indefiniteness, although they center around fulfillment of the national and individual life, and the threat is the exclusion from such fulfillment through national extinction and individual catastrophe. Faith, for the men of the Old Testament, is the state of being ultimately and unconditionally concerned about Jahweh and about what he represents in demand, threat and promise.

Another example—almost a counter-example, yet nevertheless quality revealing—is the ultimate concern with "success" and with social standing and economic power. It is the god of many people in the highly competitive Western culture and it does what every ultimate concern must do: it demands unconditional surrender to its laws even if the price is the sacrifice of genuine human relations, personal conviction, and creative *eros*. Its threat is social and economic defeat, and its promise—indefinite as all such promises—the fulfillment of one's being. It is the breakdown of this kind of faith which characterizes and makes religiously important most contemporary literature. Not false calculations but a misplaced faith is revealed in novels like *Point of No Return*. When fulfilled, the promise of this faith proves to be empty.

Faith is the state of being ultimately concerned. The content matters infinitely for the life of the believer, but it does not matter for the formal definition of faith. And this is the first step we have to make in order to understand the dynamics of faith.

2. Faith As a Centered Act

Faith as ultimate concern is an act of the total personality. It happens in the center of the personal life and includes all its elements. Faith is the most centered act of the human mind. It is not a movement of a special section or a special function of man's total being. They all are united in the act of faith. But faith is not the sum total of their impacts. It transcends every special impact as well as the totality of them and it has itself a decisive impact on each of them.

Since faith is an act of the personality as a whole, it participates in the dynamics of personal life. These dynamics have been described in many ways, especially in the recent developments of analytic psychology. Thinking in polarities, their tensions and their possible conflicts, is a common characteristic of most of them. This makes the psychology of personality highly dynamic and requires a dynamic theory of faith as the most personal of all personal acts. The first and decisive polarity in analytic psychology is that between the so-called unconscious and the conscious. Faith as an act of the total personality is not imaginable without the participation of the unconscious elements in the personality structure. They are always present and decide largely about the content of faith. But, on the other hand, faith is a conscious act and the unconscious elements participate in the creation of faith only if they are taken into the personal center which transcends each of them. If this does not happen, if unconscious forces determine the mental status without a centered act, faith does not occur, and compulsions take its place. For faith is a matter of freedom. Freedom is nothing more than the possibility of centered personal acts. The frequent discussion in which faith and freedom are contrasted could be helped by the insight that faith is a free, namely, centered act of the personality. In this respect freedom and faith are identical.

Also important for the understanding of faith is the polarity between what Freud and his school call ego and superego. The concept of the superego is quite ambiguous. On the one hand, it is the basis of all cultural life because it restricts the uninhibited actualization of the always-driving libido; on the other hand, it cuts off man's vital forces, and produces disgust about the whole system of cultural restrictions, and brings about a neurotic state of mind. From this point of view, the symbols of faith are considered to be expressions of the superego or, more concretely, to be an expression of the father image which gives content to the superego. Responsible for this inadequate theory of the superego is Freud's naturalistic negation of norms and principles. If the superego is not established through valid principles, it becomes a suppressive tyrant. But real faith, even if it uses the father image for its expression, transforms this image into a principle of truth and justice to be defended even against the "father." Faith and culture can be affirmed only if the superego represents the norms and principles of reality.

This leads to the question of how faith as a personal, centered act is related to the rational structure of man's personality which is manifest in his meaningful language, in his ability to know the true and to do the good, in his sense of beauty and justice. All this, and not only his possibility to analyze, to calculate and to argue, makes him a rational being. But in spite of this larger concept of reason we must deny that man's essential nature is identical with the rational character of his mind. Man is able to decide for or against reason, he is able to create beyond reason or to destroy below reason. This power is the power of his self, the center of self-relatedness in which all elements of his being are united. Faith is not an act of any of his rational functions, as it is not an act of the unconscious, but it is an act in which both the rational and the nonrational elements of his being are transcended.

Faith as the embracing and centered act of the personality is "ecstatic." It transcends both the drives of the nonrational unconscious and the structures of the rational conscious. It transcends them, but it does not destroy them. The ecstatic character of faith does not exclude its rational character although it is not identical with it, and it includes nonrational strivings without being identical with them. In the ecstasy of faith there is an awareness of truth and of ethical value; there are also past loves and hates, conflicts and reunions, individual and collective influences. "Ecstasy" means "standing outside of oneself"—without ceasing to be oneself—with all the elements which are united in the personal center.

A further polarity in these elements, relevant for the understanding of faith, is the tension between the cognitive function of man's personal life, on the one hand, and emotion and will, on the other hand. In a later discussion I will try to show that many distortions of the meaning of faith are rooted in the attempt to subsume faith to the one or the other of these functions. At this point it must be stated as sharply and insistently as possible that in every act of faith there is cognitive affirmation, not as the result of an independent process of inquiry but as an inseparable element in a total act of acceptance and surrender. This also excludes the idea that faith is the result of an independent act of "will to believe." There is certainly affirmation by the will of what concerns one ultimately, but faith is not a creation of the will. In the ecstasy of faith the will to accept and to surrender is an element, but not the cause. And this is true also of feeling. Faith is not an emotional outburst: this is not the meaning of ecstasy. Certainly, emotion is in it, as in every act of man's spiritual life. But emotion does not produce faith. Faith has a cognitive content and is an act of the will. It is the unity of every element in the centered self. Of course, the unity of all elements in the act of faith does not prevent one or the other element from dominating in a special form of faith. It dominates the character of faith but it does not create the act of faith.

This also answers the question of a possible psychology of faith. Everything that happens in man's personal being can become an object of psychology. And it is rather important for both the philosopher of religion and the practical minister to know how the act of faith is embedded in the totality of psychological processes. But in contrast to this justified and desirable form of a psychology of faith there is another one which tries to derive faith from something that is not faith but is most frequently fear. The presupposition of this method is that fear or something else from which faith is derived is more original and basic than faith. But this presupposition cannot be proved. On the contrary, one can prove that in the scientific method which leads to such consequences faith is already effective. Faith precedes all attempts to derive it from something else, because these attempts are themselves based on faith.

3. THE SOURCE OF FAITH

We have described the act of faith and its relation to the dynamics of personality. Faith is a total and centered act of the personal self, the act of unconditional, infinite and ultimate concern. The question now arises: what is the source of this all-embracing and all-transcending concern? The word "concern" points to two sides of a relationship, the relation between the one who is concerned and his concern. In both respects we have to imagine man's situation in itself and in his world. The reality of man's ultimate concern reveals something about his being, namely, that he is able to transcend the flux of relative and transitory experiences of his ordinary life. Man's experiences, feelings, thoughts are conditioned and finite. They not only come and go, but their content is of finite and conditional concern— unless they are elevated to unconditional validity. But this presupposes the general possibility of doing so; it presupposes the element of infinity in man. Man is able to understand in an immediate personal and central act the meaning of the ultimate, the unconditional, the absolute, the infinite. This alone makes faith a human potentiality.

Human potentialities are powers that drive toward actualization. Man is driven toward faith by his awareness of the infinite to which he belongs, but which he does not own like a possession. This is in abstract terms what concretely appears as the "restlessness of the heart" within the flux of life.

The unconditional concern which is faith is the

concern about the unconditional. The infinite passion, as faith has been described, is the passion for the infinite. Or, to use our first term, the ultimate concern is concern about what is experienced as ultimate. In this way we have turned from the subjective meaning of faith as a centered act of the personality to its objective meaning, to what is meant in the act of faith. It would not help at this point of our analysis to call that which is meant in the act of faith "God" or "a god." For at this step we ask: What in the idea of God constitutes divinity? The answer is: It is the element of the unconditional and of ultimacy. This carries the quality of divinity. If this is seen, one can understand why almost every thing "in heaven and on earth" has received ultimacy in the history of human religion. But we also can understand that a critical principle was and is at work in man's religious consciousness, namely, that which is really ultimate over against what claims to be ultimate but is only preliminary, transitory, finite.

The term "ultimate concern" unites the subjective and the objective side of the act of faith—the *fides qua creditur* (the faith through which one believes) and the *fides quae creditur* (the faith which is believed). The first is the classical term for the centered act of the personality, the ultimate concern. The second is the classical term for that toward which this act is directed, the ultimate itself, expressed in symbols of the divine. This distinction is very important, but not ultimately so, for the one side cannot be without the other. There is no faith without a content toward which it is directed. There is always something meant in the act of faith. And there is no way of having the content of faith except in the act of faith. All speaking about divine matters which is not done in the state of ultimate concern is meaningless. Because that which is meant in the act of faith cannot be approached in any other way than through an act of faith.

In terms like "ultimate," "unconditional," "infinite," "absolute," the difference between subjectivity and objectivity is overcome. The ultimate of the act of faith and the ultimate that is meant in the act of faith are one and the same. This is symbolically expressed by the mystics when they say that their knowledge of God is the knowledge God has of himself; and it is expressed by Paul when he says (I Cor. 13) that he will know as he is known, namely, by God. God never can be object without being at the same time subject. Even a successful prayer is, according to Paul (Rom. 8), not possible without God as Spirit praying within us. The same experience expressed in abstract language is the disappearance of the ordinary subject-object scheme in the experience of the ultimate, the unconditional. In the act of faith that which is the source of this act is present beyond the cleavage of subject and object. It is present as both and beyond both.

This character of faith gives an additional criterion for distinguishing true and false ultimacy. The finite which claims infinity without having it (as, e.g., a nation or success) is not able to transcend the subject-object scheme. It remains an object which the believer looks at as a subject. He can approach it with ordinary knowledge and subject it to ordinary handling. There are, of course, many degrees in the endless realm of false ultimacies. The nation is nearer to true ultimacy than is success. Nationalistic ecstasy can produce a state in which the subject is almost swallowed by the object. But after a period the subject emerges again, disappointed radically and totally, and by looking at the nation in a skeptical and calculating way does injustice even to its justified claims. The more idolatrous a faith the less it is able to overcome the cleavage between subject and object. For that is the difference between true and idolatrous faith. In true faith the ultimate concern is a concern about the truly ultimate; while in idolatrous faith preliminary, finite realities are elevated to the rank of ultimacy. The inescapable consequence of idolatrous faith is "existential disappointment," a disappointment which penetrates into the very existence of man! This is the dynamics of idolatrous faith: that it is faith, and as such, the centered act of a personality; that the entering point is something which is more or less on the periphery; and that, therefore, the act of faith leads to a loss of the center and to a disruption of the personality. The ecstatic character of even an idolatrous faith can hide this consequence only for a certain time. But finally it breaks into the open.

4. FAITH AND THE DYNAMICS OF THE HOLY

He who enters the sphere of faith enters the sanctuary of life. Where there is faith there is an awareness of holiness. This seems to contradict what has just been said about idolatrous faith. But it does not contradict our analysis of idolatry. It only contradicts the popular way in which the word "holy" is used. What concerns one ultimately becomes holy. The awareness of the holy is awareness of the presence of the divine, namely of the content of our ultimate concern. This awareness is expressed in a grand way in the Old Testament from the visions of the patriarchs and Moses to the shaking experiences of the great prophets and psalmists. It is a presence which remains mysterious in spite of its appearance, and it exercises both an attractive and a repulsive function on those who encounter it. In his classical book, *The Idea of the Holy,* Rudolph Otto has described these two functions as the fascinating and the shaking character of the holy. (In Otto's terminology: *mysterium fascinans et tremendum.*) They can be found in all religions because they are the way in which man always encounters the representations of his ultimate concern. The reason for these two effects of the holy is obvious if we see the relation of the experience of the holy to the experience of ultimate concern. The human heart seeks the infinite because that is where the finite wants to rest. In the infinite it sees its own fulfillment. This is the reason for the ecstatic attraction and fascination of everything in which ultimacy is manifest. On the other hand, if ultimacy is manifest and exercises its fascinating attraction, one realizes at the same time the infinite distance of the finite from the infinite and, consequently, the negative judgment over any finite attempts to reach the infinite. The feeling of being consumed in the presence of the divine is a profound expression of man's relation to the holy. It is implied in every genuine act of faith, in every state of ultimate concern.

This original and only justified meaning of holiness must replace the currently distorted use of the word. "Holy" has become identified with moral perfection, especially in some Protestant groups. The historical causes of this distortion give a new insight into the nature of holiness and of faith. Originally, the holy has meant what is apart from the ordinary realm of things and experiences. It is separated from the world of finite relations. This is the reason why all religious cults have separated holy places and activities from all other places and activities. Entering the sanctuary means encountering the holy. Here the infinitely removed makes itself near and present, without losing its remoteness. For this reason, the holy has been called the "entirely other," namely, other than the ordinary course of things or—to refer to a former statement—other than the world which is determined by the cleavage of subject and object. The holy transcends this realm; this is its mystery and its unapproachable character. There is no conditional way of reaching the unconditional; there is no finite way of reaching the infinite.

The mysterious character of the holy produces an ambiguity in man's ways of experiencing it. The holy can appear as creative and as destructive. Its fascinating element can be both creative and destructive (referring again to the fascinating character of the nationalistic idolatry), and the terrifying and consuming element can be destructive and creative (as in the double function of Siva or Kali in Indian thought). This ambiguity, of which we still find traces in the Old Testament, is reflected in the ritual or quasi-ritual activities of religions and quasi religions (sacrifices of others or one's bodily or mental self) which are strongly ambiguous. One can call this ambiguity divine-demonic, whereby the divine is characterized by the victory of the creative over the destructive possibility of the holy, and the demonic is characterized by the victory of the destructive over the creative possibility of the holy. In this situation, which is most profoundly understood in the prophetic religion of the Old Testament, a fight has been waged against the demonic-destructive element in the holy. And this fight was so successful that the concept of the holy was changed. Holiness becomes justice and truth. It is creative and not destructive. The true sacrifice is obedience to the law. This is the line of thought which finally led to the identification of holiness with moral perfection. But when this point is reached, holiness loses its meaning as the "separated," the "transcending," the "fascinating and terrifying," the "entirely other." All this is gone, and the holy has become the morally good and the logically true. It has ceased to be the holy in the genuine sense of the word. Summing up this development, one could say that the holy originally lies below the alternative of the good and the evil; that it is both divine and demonic; that with the reduction of the demonic possibility the holy itself becomes transformed in its meaning; that it becomes rational and identical with the true and the

good; and that its genuine meaning must be redis-
covered.

These dynamics of the holy confirm what was
said about the dynamics of faith. We have distinguished between true and idolatrous faith. The holy
which is demonic, or ultimately destructive, is identical with the content of idolatrous faith. Idolatrous
faith is still faith. The holy which is demonic is still
holy. This is the point where the ambiguous character of religion is most visible and the dangers of faith
are most obvious: the danger of faith is idolatry and
the ambiguity of the holy is its demonic possibility.
Our ultimate concern can destroy us as it can heal
us. But we never can be without it.

5. FAITH AND DOUBT

We now return to a fuller description of faith as an
act of the human personality, as its centered and
total act. An act of faith is an act of a finite being
who is grasped by and turned to the infinite. It is a
finite act with all the limitations of a finite act, and it
is an act in which the infinite participates beyond the
limitations of a finite act. Faith is certain in so far as
it is an experience of the holy. But faith is uncertain
in so far as the infinite to which it is related is
received by a finite being. This element of uncertainty in faith cannot be removed, it must be

accepted. And the element in faith which accepts this is courage. Faith includes an element of immediate awareness which gives certainty and an element of uncertainty. To accept this is courage. In the courageous standing of uncertainty, faith shows most visibly its dynamic character.

If we try to describe the relation of faith and courage, we must use a larger concept of courage than that which is ordinarily used.* Courage as an element of faith is the daring self-affirmation of one's own being in spite of the powers of "nonbeing" which are the heritage of everything finite. Where there is daring and courage there is the possibility of failure. And in every act of faith this possibility is present. The risk must be taken. Whoever makes his nation his ultimate concern needs courage in order to maintain this concern. Only certain is the ultimacy as ultimacy, the infinite passion as infinite passion. This is a reality given to the self with his own nature. It is as immediate and as much beyond doubt as the self is to the self. It *is* the self in its self-transcending quality. But there is not certainty of this kind about the content of our ultimate concern, be it nation, success, a god, or the God of the Bible: They all are contents without immediate awareness. Their acceptance as matters of ultimate concern is a

---

*Cf. Paul Tillich, *The Courage to Be*. Yale University Press.

risk and therefore an act of courage. There is a risk if what was considered as a matter of ultimate concern proves to be a matter of preliminary and transitory concern—as, for example, the nation. The risk to faith in one's ultimate concern is indeed the greatest risk man can run. For if it proves to be a failure, the meaning of one's life breaks down; one surrenders oneself, including truth and justice, to something which is not worth it. One has given away one's personal center without having a chance to regain it. The reaction of despair in people who have experienced the breakdown of their national claims is an irrefutable proof of the idolatrous character of their national concern. In the long run this is the inescapable result of an ultimate concern, the subject matter of which is not ultimate. And this is the risk faith must take; this is the risk which is unavoidable if a finite being affirms itself. Ultimate concern is ultimate risk and ultimate courage. It is not risk and needs no courage with respect to ultimacy itself. But it is risk and demands courage if it affirms a concrete concern. And every faith has a concrete element in itself. It is concerned about something or somebody. But this something or this somebody may prove to be not ultimate at all. Then faith is a failure in its concrete expression, although it it not a failure in the experience of the unconditional itself. A god disappears; divinity remains. Faith risks the vanishing of the concrete god in whom it believes. It may well be that with the vanishing of the god the believer breaks down without being able to re-establish his centered self by a new content of his ultimate concern. This risk cannot be taken away from any act of faith. There is only one point which is a matter not of risk but of immediate certainty and herein lies the greatness and the pain of being human; namely, one's standing between one's finitude and one's potential infinity.

All this is sharply expressed in the relation of faith and doubt. If faith is understood as belief that something is true, doubt is incompatible with the act of faith. If faith is understood as being ultimately concerned, doubt is a necessary element in it. It is a consequence of the risk of faith.

The doubt which is implicit in faith is not a doubt about facts or conclusions. It is not the same doubt which is the lifeblood of scientific research. Even the most orthodox theologian does not deny the right of methodological doubt in matters of empirical inquiry or logical deduction. A scientist who would say that a scientific theory is beyond doubt would at that moment cease to be scientific. He may believe that the theory can be trusted for all practical purposes. Without such belief no technical application of a theory would be possible. One could attribute to this kind of belief pragmatic certainty sufficient for action. Doubt in this case points to the preliminary character of the underlying theory.

There is another kind of doubt, which we could call skeptical in contrast to the scientific doubt which we could call methodological. The skeptical doubt is an attitude toward all the beliefs of man, from sense experiences to religious creeds. It is more an attitude than an assertion. For as an assertion it would conflict with itself. Even the assertion that there is no possible truth for man would be judged by the skeptical principle and could not stand as an assertion. Genuine skeptical doubt does not use the form of an assertion. It is an attitude of actually rejecting any certainty. Therefore, it cannot be refuted logically. It does not transform its attitude into a proposition. Such an attitude necessarily leads either to despair or cynicism, or to both alternately. And often, if this alternative becomes intolerable, it leads to indifference and the attempt to develop an attitude of complete unconcern. But since man is that being who is essentially concerned about his being, such an escape finally breaks down. This is the dynamics of skeptical doubt. It has an awakening and liberating function, but it also can prevent the development of a centered personality. For personality is not possible without faith. The despair about truth by the skeptic shows that truth is still his infinite passion. The cynical superiority over every concrete truth shows that truth is still taken seriously and that the impact of the question of an ultimate concern is strongly felt. The skeptic, so long as he is a serious skeptic, is not without faith, even though it has no concrete content.

The doubt which is implicit in every act of faith is neither the methodological nor the skeptical doubt. It is the doubt which accompanies every risk. It is not the permanent doubt of the scientist, and it is not the transitory doubt of the skeptic, but it is the doubt of him who is ultimately concerned about a concrete content. One could call it the existential doubt, in contrast to the methodological and the skeptical doubt. It does not question whether a special proposition is true or false. It does not reject every concrete truth, but it is aware of the element of insecurity in every existential truth. At the same time, the doubt which is implied in faith accepts this insecurity and takes it into itself in an act of courage. Faith includes courage. Therefore, it can include the doubt about itself. Certainly faith and courage are not identical. Faith has other elements besides courage and courage has other functions beyond affirming faith. Nevertheless, an act in which courage accepts risk belongs to the dynamics of faith.

This dynamic concept of faith seems to give no place to that restful affirmative confidence which we find in the documents of all great religions, including Christianity. But this is not the case. The dynamic concept of faith is the result of a conceptual analysis, both of the subjective and of the objective side of faith. It is by no means the description of an always actualized state of the mind. An analysis of structure is not the description of a state of things. The confusion of these two is a source of many misunderstandings and errors in all realms of life. An example, taken from the current discussion of anxiety, is typical of this confusion. The description of anxiety as the awareness of one's finitude is sometimes criticized as untrue from the point of view of the ordinary state of the mind. Anxiety, one says, appears under special conditions but is not an ever-present implication of man's finitude. Certainly anxiety as an acute experience appears under definite conditions. But the underlying structure of finite life is the universal condition which makes the appearance of anxiety under special conditions possible. In the same way doubt is not a permanent experience within the act of faith. But it is always present as an element in the structure of faith. This is the difference between faith and immediate evidence either of perceptual or of logical character. There is no faith without an intrinsic "in spite of" and the courageous affirmation of oneself in the state of ultimate concern. This intrinsic element of doubt breaks into the open under special individual and social conditions. If doubt appears, it should not be considered as the negation of faith, but as an element which was always and will always be present in the act of faith. Existential doubt and faith are poles of the same reality, the state of ultimate concern.

The insight into this structure of faith and doubt is of tremendous practical importance. Many Christians, as well as members of other religious groups, feel anxiety, guilt and despair about what they call "loss of faith." But serious doubt is confirmation of faith. It indicates the seriousness of the concern, its unconditional character. This also refers to those who as future or present ministers of a church experience not only scientific doubt about doctrinal statements—this is as necessary and perpetual as theology is a perpetual need—but also existential doubt about the message of their church, e.g., that Jesus can be called the Christ. The criterion according to which they should judge themselves is the seriousness and ultimacy of their concern about the content of both their faith and their doubt.

6. FAITH AND COMMUNITY

The last remarks about faith and doubt in relation to religious creeds have led us to those problems which are ordinarily dominant in the popular mind in the discussion of faith. Faith is seen in its doctrinal formulations or in its legally dogmatic expressions. It is seen in its sociological setting more than in its character as a personal act. The historical causes of this attitude are obvious. The periods of suppression of the autonomous mind, culturally and religiously, in the name of the doctrinal formulations of a special faith, are remembered by the following generations. The life-and-death struggle of rebellious autonomy with the powers of religious suppression has left a deep scar in the "collective unconscious." This is true even in the present period, when the kind of suppression that existed at the end of the Middle Ages and in the period of the religious wars is a thing of the past. Therefore, it is not futile to defend the dynamic concept of faith against the accusation that it would lead back to new forms of orthodoxy and religious suppression. Certainly, if doubt is considered an intrinsic element of faith, the autonomous creativity of the human mind is in no way restricted. But, one will ask, is not this concept of faith incompatible with the "community of faith" which is a decisive reality in all religions? Is not the dynamic idea of faith an expression of Protestant individualism and humanistic autonomy? Can a community of faith—e.g., a church—accept a faith which includes doubt as an intrinsic element and calls the seriousness of doubt an expression of faith?

And even if it could allow such an attitude in its ordinary members, how could it permit the same in its leaders?

The answers to these often rather passionately asked questions are many-sided and involved. At the present point the obvious and yet significant assertion must be made that the act of faith, like every act in man's spiritual life, is dependent on language and therefore on community. For only in the community of spiritual beings is language alive. Without language there is no act of faith, no religious experience! This refers to language generally and to the special language in every function of man's spiritual life. The religious language, the language of symbol and myth, is created in the community of the believers and cannot be fully understood outside this community. But within it, the religious language enables the act of faith to have a concrete content. Faith needs its language, as does every act of the personality; without language it would be blind, not directed toward a content, not conscious of itself. This is the reason for the predominant significance of the community of faith. Only as a member of such a community (even if in isolation or expulsion) can man have a content for his ultimate concern. Only in a community of language can man actualize his faith.

But now one will repeat the question and ask: If there is no faith without community of faith, is it not necessary that the community formulate the content of its faith in a definite way as a creedal statement and demand that every member of the community accept it? Certainly this is the way in which the creeds came into existence. This is the reason for their dogmatic and legal fixation! But this does not explain the tremendous power of these expressions of the communal faith over groups and individuals from generation to generation. Nor does it explain the fanatacism with which doubts and deviations were suppressed, not only by external power but even more by the mechanisms of inner suppression. These mechanisms had been planted into the individual mind and were most effective even without pressure from outside. In order to understand these facts we must remember that faith as the state of ultimate concern includes total surrender to the content of this concern in a centered act of the personality. This means that the existence of the personality in the ultimate sense is at stake. Idolatrous concern and devotion may destroy the center of the personality. If, as in the Christian Church, in centuries of strife the content of the communal faith has been defended against idolatrous intrusions and has been formulated as a defense against such intrusions, it is understandable that every deviation from these formulations is considered destructive for the "soul" of the Christian.

He is thought to have fallen under demonic influences. Ecclesiastical punishments are attempts to save him from demonic self-destruction. In these measures the concern which is the content of faith is taken absolutely seriously. It is a matter of eternal life and death.

But it is not only the individual for whom subjection to the established creed is of decisive importance. It is also the community of faith as such which must be protected against the distorting influences of individuals. The Church excludes from its community those who are thought to have denied the foundations of the Church. This is the meaning of the concept of "heresy." The heretic is not one who has erroneous beliefs (this is a possible implication of heresy, but not its essence), but the heretic is one who has turned away from the true to a false, idolatrous concern. Therefore, he may influence others in the same direction, destroy them, and undermine the community. If the civil authorities consider the Church as the basis of the conformity and cultural substance without which a society cannot live, they persecute the heretic as a civil criminal and use means of indoctrination and external pressure by which they try to keep the unity of the religio-political realm. However, if this point is reached, the reaction of man's spiritual autonomy begins to work and, if victorious, removes not only the political enforcement of a creedal system but the creedal system itself—and, beyond this, often faith itself. But this proves to be impossible. It can be and has always been done only through the power of another ultimate concern. Faith stands against faith in the world's historical struggles between the Church and its liberal critics. Even the faith of the liberal needs expression and some communal formulation, and it needs to be defended against authoritarian attacks. Even more: the ultimate concern of the liberal needs concrete contents, as does every ultimate concern. He also lives in institutions of a definite historical character. He, too, has a special language and uses special symbols. His faith is not the abstract affirmation of freedom, but is the faith in freedom as an element in the concreteness of a total situation. If he undercuts this concreteness in the name of freedom, he produces a vacuum into which antiliberal forces easily enter. Only creative faith can resist the onslaught of destructive faith. Only the concern with what is truly ultimate can stand against idolatrous concerns.

All this drives to the question: How is a community of faith possible without suppression of the autonomy of man's spiritual life? The first answer is based on the relation of the civil authorities to the community of faith. Even if a society is practically identical with a community of faith and the actual

life of the group is determined by the spiritual substance of a church, the civil authorities should as
such remain neutral and risk the rise of dissident
forms of faith. If they try to enforce spiritual conformity, and are successful, they have removed the
risk and courage which belong to the act of faith.
They have transformed faith into a behavior pattern
which does not admit alternatives, and which loses
its character of ultimacy even if the fulfillment of the
religious duties is done with ultimate concern.
However, such a situation has become rare in our
period. In most societies the civil authorities have to
deal with different communities of faith, unable to
enforce the one or the other in all members of the
society. In this case the spiritual substance of the
social group is determined by the common denominator of the different groups and their common tradition. This denominator may be more secular or
more religious. In any case it is an outgrowth of
faith, and its expression—as in the American Consti-
tution—is affirmed in an attitude which sometimes
has the unconditional character of an ultimate
concern, but more often the conditional character
of a preliminary concern of highest degree. Just for
this reason the civil authorities should not try to
prohibit the expression of doubt about such a basic
law, although they must enforce the legal consequences of it.

The second step in the solution of the problem deals with faith and doubt within the community of faith itself. The question is whether the dynamic concept of faith is incompatible with a community which needs creedal expressions of the concrete elements in its ultimate concern. The answer which follows from the preceding analyses is that no answer is possible if the character of the creed excludes the presence of doubt. The concept of the "infallibility" of a decision by a council or a bishop or a book excludes doubt as an element of faith in those who subject themselves to these authorities. They may have to struggle within themselves about their subjection; but after they have made the decision, no doubt can be admitted by them about the infallible statements of the authorities. This faith has become static, a nonquestioning surrender not only to the ultimate, which is affirmed in the act of faith, but also to its concrete elements as formulated by the religious authorities. In this way something preliminary and conditional—the human interpretation of the content of faith from the Biblical writers to the present—receives ultimacy and is elevated above the risk of doubt. The fight against the idolatrous implication of this kind of static faith was waged first by Protestantism and then, when Protestantism itself became static, by Enlightenment. This protest, however insufficient its expression, aimed originally at a dynamic faith and not at the negation of faith, not even at the negation of creedal formulations. So we stand again before the question: How can a faith which has doubt as an element within itself be united with creedal statements of the community of faith? The answer can only be that creedal expressions of the ultimate concern of the community must include their own criticism. It must become obvious in all of them—be they liturgical, doctrinal or ethical expressions of the faith of the community—that they are not ultimate. Rather, their function is to point to the ultimate which is beyond all of them. This is what I call the "Protestant principle," the critical element in the expression of the community of faith and consequently the element of doubt in the act of faith. Neither the doubt nor the critical element is always actual, but both must always be possible within the circle of faith. From the Christian point of view, one would say that the Church with all its doctrines and institutions and authorities stands under the prophetic judgment and not above it. Criticism and doubt show that the community of faith stands "under the Cross," if the Cross is understood as the divine judgment over man's religious life, and even over Christianity, though it has accepted the sign of the Cross. In this way the dynamic faith which we first have described in personal terms is applied to the community of faith. Certainly, the life of a community of faith is a continuous risk, if faith itself is understood as a risk. But this is the character of dynamic faith, and the consequence of the Protestant principle.

II

WHAT FAITH IS NOT

1. THE INTELLECTUALISTIC DISTORTION OF THE MEANING OF FAITH

Our positive description of what faith is implies the rejection of interpretations that dangerously distort the meaning of faith. It is necessary to make these implicit rejections explicit, because the distortions exercise a tremendous power over popular thinking and have been largely responsible for alienating many from religion since the beginning of the scientific age. It is not only the popular mind which distorts the meaning of faith. Behind it lie philosophical and theological thoughts which in a more refined way also miss the meaning of faith.

The different distorted interpretations of the meaning of faith can be traced to one source. Faith as being ultimately concerned is a centered act of the whole personality. If one of the functions which constitute the totality of the personality is partly or completely identified with faith, the meaning of faith is distorted. Such interpretations are not altogether wrong because every function of the human mind participates in the act of faith. But the element of truth in them is embedded in a whole of error.

The most ordinary misinterpretation of faith is to consider it an act of knowledge that has a low degree of evidence. Something more or less probable or improbable is affirmed in spite of the insufficiency of its theoretical substantiation. This situation is very usual in daily life. If this is meant, one is speaking of *belief* rather than of faith. One believes that one's information is correct. One believes that records of past events are useful for the reconstruction of facts. One believes that a scientific theory is adequate for the understanding of a series of facts. One believes that a person will act in a specific way or that a political situation will change in a certain direction. In all these cases the belief is based on evidence sufficient to make the event probable. Sometimes, however, one believes something which has low probability or is strictly improbable, though not impossible. The causes for all these theoretical and practical beliefs are rather varied. Some things are believed because we have good though not complete evidence about them; many more things are believed because they are stated by good authorities. This is the case whenever we accept the evidence which others accepted as sufficient for belief, even if we cannot approach the evidence directly (for example, all events of the past). Here a new element comes into the picture, namely, the trust in the authority which makes a statement probable for us. Without such trust we could not believe anything except the objects of our immediate experience. The consequence would be that our world would be infinitely smaller than it actually is. It is rational to trust in authorities which enlarge our consciousness without forcing us into submission. If we use the word "faith" for this kind of trust we can say that most of our knowledge is based on faith. But it is not appropriate to do so. We believe the authorities, we trust their judgment, though never uncondition- ally, but we do not have faith in them. Faith is more than trust in authorities, although trust is an ele- ment of faith. This distinction is important in view of the fact that some earlier theologians tried to prove the unconditional authority of the Biblical writers by showing their trustworthiness as wit- nesses. The Christian may believe the Biblical writ- ers, but not unconditionally. He does not have faith in them. He should not even have faith in the Bible. For faith is more than trust in even the most sacred authority. It is participation in the subject of one's ultimate concern with one's whole being. Therefore, the term "faith" should not be used in connection with theoretical knowledge, whether it is a knowledge on the basis of immediate, prescientific or scientific evidence, or whether it is on the basis of trust in authorities who themselves are dependent on direct or indirect evidence.

The terminological inquiry has led us into the material problem itself. Faith does not affirm or deny what belongs to the prescientific or scientific knowledge of our world, whether we know it by direct experience or through the experience of others. The knowledge of our world (including ourselves as a part of the world) is a matter of inquiry by ourselves or by those in whom we trust. It is not a matter of faith. The dimension of faith is not the dimension of science, history or psychology. The acceptance of a probable hypothesis in these realms is not faith, but preliminary belief, to be tested by scholarly methods and to be changed by every new discovery. Almost all the struggles between faith and knowledge are rooted in the wrong understanding of faith as a type of knowledge which has a low degree of evidence but is supported by religious authority. It is, however, not only confusion of faith with knowledge that is responsible for the world historical conflicts between them; it is also the fact that matters of faith in the sense of ultimate concern lie hidden behind an assumedly scientific method. Whenever this happens, faith stands against faith and not against knowledge.

The difference between faith and knowledge is also visible in the kind of certitude each gives. There are two types of knowledge which are based on complete evidence and give complete certitude. The one is the immediate evidence of sense perception. He who sees a green color sees a green color and is certain about it. He cannot be certain whether the thing which seems to him green is really green. He may be under a deception. But he cannot doubt that he sees green. The other complete evidence is that of the logical and mathematical rules which are presupposed even if their formulation admits different and sometimes conflicting methods. One cannot discuss logic without presupposing those implicit rules which make the discussion meaningful. Here we have absolute certitude; but we have no reality, just as in the case of mere sense perception. Nevertheless, this certitude is not without value. No truth is possible without the material given by sense perception and without the form given by the logical and mathematical rules which express the structure in which all reality stands. One of the worst errors of theology and popular religion is to make statements which intentionally or unintentionally contradict the structure of reality. Such an attitude is an expression not of faith but of the confusion of faith with belief.

Knowledge of reality has never the certitude of complete evidence. The process of knowing is infinite. It never comes to an end except in a state of knowledge of the whole. But such knowledge transcends infinitely every finite mind and can be ascribed only to God. Every knowledge of reality by the human mind has the character of higher or lower probability. The certitude about a physical law, a historical fact, or a psychological structure can be so high that, for all practical purposes, it is certain. But theoretically the incomplete certitude of belief remains and can be undercut at any moment by criticism and new experience. The certitude of faith has not this character. Neither has it the character of formal evidence. The certitude of faith is "existential," meaning that the whole existence of man is involved. It has, as we indicated before, two elements: the one, which is not a risk but a certainty about one's own being, namely, on being related to something ultimate or unconditional; the other, which is a risk and involves doubt and courage, namely, the surrender to a concern which is not really ultimate and may be destructive if taken as ultimate. This is not a theoretical problem of the kind of higher or lower evidence, of probability or improbability, but it is an existential problem of "to be or not to be." It belongs to a dimension other than any theoretical judgment. Faith is not belief and it is not knowledge with a low degree of probability. Its certitude is not the uncertain certitude of a theoretical judgment.

2. THE VOLUNTARISTIC DISTORTION OF THE MEANING OF FAITH

One can divide this form of the distorted interpretation of faith into a Catholic and a Protestant type. The Catholic type has a great tradition in the Roman Church. It goes back to Thomas Aquinas, who emphasized that the lack of evidence which faith has must be complemented by an act of will. This, first of all, presupposes that faith is understood as an act of knowledge with a limited evidence and that the lack of evidence is made up by an act of will. We have seen that this way of understanding faith does not do justice to the existential character of faith. Our criticism of the intellectualistic distortion of the meaning of faith hits basically also the voluntaristic distortion of the meaning of faith. The former is the basis of the latter. Without a theoretically formulated content the "will to believe" would be empty. But the content which is meant in the will to believe is given to the will by the intellect. For instance, someone has doubts about the so-called "immortality of the soul." He realizes that this assertion that the soul continues to live after the death of the body cannot be proved either by evidence or by trustworthy authority. It is a questionable proposition of theoretical character. But there are motives driving people to this assertion. They decide to believe, and make up in this way for the lack of evidence. If this belief is called "faith," it is a misnomer, even if much evidence were collected for the belief in a continuation of life after death. In classical Roman Catholic theology the "will to believe" is not an act which originates in man's striving, but it is given by grace to him whose will is moved by God to accept the truth of what the Church teaches. Even so, it is not the intellect which is determined by its content to believe, but it is the will which performs what the intellect alone cannot do. This kind of interpretation agrees with the authoritarian attitude of the Roman Church. For it is the authority of the Church which gives the contents, to be affirmed by the intellect under the impact of the will. If the idea of grace mediated by the Church and motivating the will is rejected, as in pragmatism, the will to believe becomes willfulness. It becomes an arbitrary decision which may be supported by some insufficient arguments but which could have gone in other directions with equal justification. Such belief as the basis of the will to believe is certainly not faith.

The Protestant form of the will to believe is connected with the moral interpretation of religion by Protestants. One demands "obedience of faith," following a Paulinian phrase. The term can mean two different things. It can mean the element of commitment which is implied in the state of ultimate concern. If this is meant, one simply says that in the state of ultimate concern all mental functions participate— which certainly is true. Or the term "obedience of faith" can mean subjection to the command to believe as it is given in prophetic and apostolic preaching. Certainly, if a prophetic word is accepted as prophetic, i.e., as coming from God, obedience of faith does not mean anything other than accepting a message as coming from God. But if there is doubt whether a "word" is prophetic, the term "obedience of faith" loses its meaning. It becomes an arbitrary "will to believe." Yet one may describe the situation in a more refined way and point to the fact that we are often grasped by something, e.g., Biblical passages, as expressions of the objectively ultimate concern, but we hesitate to accept them as our subjective ultimate concern for escapist reasons. In such cases, one says, the appeal to the will is justified and does not ask for a willful decision. This is true; but such an act of will does not produce faith—faith as ultimate concern is already given. The demand to be obedient is the demand to be what one already is, namely, committed to the ultimate concern from which one tries to escape. Only if this is the situation can obedience of faith be demanded; but then faith precedes the obedience and is not the product of it. No command to believe and no will to believe can create faith.

This is important for religious education, counseling and preaching. One should never convey the impression to those whom one wants to impress, that faith is a demand made upon them, the rejection of which is lack of good will. Finite man cannot produce infinite concern. Our oscillating will cannot produce the certainty which belongs to faith. This is in strict analogy to what we said about the impossibility of reaching the truth of faith by arguments and authorities, which in the best case give finite knowledge of a more or less probable character. Neither arguments for belief nor the will to believe can create faith.

3. THE EMOTIONALISTIC DISTORTION OF THE MEANING OF FAITH

The difficulty of understanding faith either as a matter of the intellect or as a matter of will, or of both in mutual support, has led to the interpretation of faith as emotion. This solution was, and partly is, supported from both the religious and the secular side. For the defenders of religion it was a retreat to a seemingly safe position after the battle about faith as a matter of knowledge or will had been lost.

The father of all modern Protestant theology, Sch-leiermacher, has described religion as the feeling of unconditional dependence. Of course, feeling so defined does not mean in religion what it means in popular psychology. It is not vague and changing, but has a definite content: unconditional depen-dence, a phrase related to what we have called ulti-mate concern. Nevertheless, the word "feeling" has induced many people to believe that faith is a matter of merely subjective emotions, without a content to be known and a demand to be obeyed.

This interpretation of faith was readily accepted by representatives of science and ethics, because they took it as the best way to get rid of interference from the side of religion in the processes of scientific research and technical organization. If religion is mere feeling it is innocuous. The old conflicts between religion and culture are finished. Culture goes its way, directed by scientific knowledge, and religion is the private affair of every individual and a mere mirror of his emotional life. No claims for truth can be made by it. No competition with science, his-tory, psychology, politics is possible. Religion, put safely into the corner of subjective feelings, has lost its danger for man's cultural activities.

Neither of the two sides, the religious and the cultural, could keep this well-defined covenant of peace. Faith as the state of ultimate concern claims the whole man and cannot be restricted to the subjectivity of mere feeling. It claims truth for its concern and commitment to it. It does not accept the situation "in the corner" of mere feeling. If the whole man is grasped, all his functions are grasped. If this claim of religion is denied, religion itself is denied. It was not only religion which could not accept the restriction of faith to feeling. It was also not accepted by those who were especially interested in pushing religion into the emotional corner. Scientists, artists, moralists showed clearly that they also were ultimately concerned. Their concern expressed itself even in those creations in which they wanted most radically to deny religion. A keen analysis of most philosophical, scientific and ethical systems shows how much ultimate concern is present in them, even if they are leading in the fight against what they call religion.

This shows the limits of the emotionalist definition of faith. Certainly faith as an act of the whole personality has strong emotional elements within it. Emotion always expressed the involvement of the whole personality in an act of life or spirit. But emotion is not the source of faith. Faith is definite in its direction and concrete in its content. Therefore, it claims truth and commitment. It is directed toward the unconditional, and appears in a concrete reality that demands and justifies such commitment.

III

⊠

SYMBOLS OF FAITH

1. THE MEANING OF SYMBOL

Man's ultimate concern must be expressed symbolically, because symbolic language alone is able to
express the ultimate. This statement demands expla-
nation in several respects. In spite of the manifold
research about the meaning and function of symbols
which is going on in contemporary philosophy,
every writer who uses the term "symbol" must
explain his understanding of it.

Symbols have one characteristic in common
with signs; they point beyond themselves to something else. The red sign at the street corner points
to the order to stop the movements of cars at certain
intervals. A red light and the stopping of cars have
essentially no relation to each other, but conven-

tionally they are united as long as the convention lasts. The same is true of letters and numbers and partly even words. They point beyond themselves to sounds and meanings. They are given this special function by convention within a nation or by international conventions, as the mathematical signs. Sometimes such signs are called symbols; but this is unfortunate because it makes the distinction between signs and symbols more difficult. Decisive is the fact that signs do not participate in the reality of that to which they point, while symbols do. Therefore, signs can be replaced for reasons of expediency or convention, while symbols cannot.

This leads to the second characteristic of the symbol: It participates in that to which it points: the flag participates in the power and dignity of the nation for which it stands. Therefore, it cannot be replaced except after an historic catastrophe that changes the reality of the nation which it symbolizes. An attack on the flag is felt as an attack on the majesty of the group in which it is acknowledged. Such an attack is considered blasphemy.

The third characteristic of a symbol is that it opens up levels of reality which otherwise are closed for us. All arts create symbols for a level of reality which cannot be reached in any other way. A picture and a poem reveal elements of reality which cannot be approached scientifically. In the creative work of art we encounter reality in a dimension which is closed for us without such works. The symbol's fourth characteristic not only opens up dimensions and elements of reality which otherwise would remain unapproachable but also unlocks dimensions and elements of our soul which correspond to the dimensions and elements of reality. A great play gives us not only a new vision of the human scene, but it opens up hidden depths of our own being. Thus we are able to receive what the play reveals to us in reality. There are within us dimensions of which we cannot become aware except through symbols, as melodies and rhythms in music.

Symbols cannot be produced intentionally— this is the fifth characteristic. They grow out of the individual or collective unconscious and cannot function without being accepted by the unconscious dimension of our being. Symbols which have an especially social function, as political and religious symbols, are created or at least accepted by the collective unconscious of the group in which they appear.

The sixth and last characteristic of the symbol is a consequence of the fact that symbols cannot be invented. Like living beings, they grow and they die. They grow when the situation is ripe for them, and they die when the situation changes. The symbol of the "king" grew in a special period of history, and it died in most parts of the world in our period. Symbols do not grow because people are longing for them, and they do not die because of scientific or practical criticism. They die because they can no longer produce response in the group where they originally found expression.

These are the main characteristics of every symbol. Genuine symbols are created in several spheres of man's cultural creativity. We have mentioned already the political and the artistic realm. We could add history and, above all, religion, whose symbols will be our particular concern.

2. Religious Symbols

We have discussed the meaning of symbols generally because, as we said, man's ultimate concern must be expressed symbolically! One may ask: Why can it not be expressed directly and properly? If money, success or the nation is someone's ultimate concern, can this not be said in a direct way without symbolic language? Is it not only in those cases in which the content of the ultimate concern is called "God" that we are in the realm of symbols? The answer is that everything which is a matter of unconditional concern is made into a god. If the nation is someone's ultimate concern, the name of the nation becomes a sacred name and the nation receives divine qualities which far surpass the reality of the being and functioning of the nation. The nation then stands for and symbolizes the true ultimate, but in an idolatrous way. Success as ultimate concern is not the natural desire of actualizing potentialities, but is readiness to sacrifice all other values of life for the sake of a position of power and social predominance. The anxiety about not being a success is an idolatrous form of the anxiety about divine condemnation. Success is grace; lack of success, ultimate judgment. In this way concepts designating ordinary realities become idolatrous symbols of ultimate concern.

The reason for this transformation of concepts into symbols is the character of ultimacy and the nature of faith. That which is the true ultimate transcends the realm of finite reality infinitely. Therefore, no finite reality can express it directly and properly. Religiously speaking, God transcends his own name. This is why the use of his name easily becomes an abuse or a blasphemy. Whatever we say about that which concerns us ultimately, whether or not we call it God, has a symbolic meaning. It points beyond itself while participating in that to which it points. In no other way can faith express itself adequately. The language of faith is the language of symbols. If faith were what we have shown that it is not, such an assertion could not be made. But faith, understood as the state of being ultimately concerned, has no language other than symbols. When saying this I always expect the question: Only a symbol? He who asks this question shows that he has not understood the difference between signs and symbols nor the power of symbolic language, which surpasses in quality and strength the power of any nonsymbolic language. One should never say "only a symbol," but one should say "not less than a symbol." With this in mind we can now describe the different kinds of symbols of faith.

The fundamental symbol of our ultimate concern is God. It is always present in any act of faith, even if the act of faith includes the denial of God. Where there is ultimate concern, God can be denied only in the name of God. One God can deny the other one. Ultimate concern cannot deny its own character as ultimate. Therefore, it affirms what is meant by the word "God." Atheism, consequently, can only mean the attempt to remove any ultimate concern—to remain unconcerned about the meaning of one's existence. Indifference toward the ultimate question is the only imaginable form of atheism. Whether it is possible is a problem which must remain unsolved at this point. In any case, he who denies God as a matter of ultimate concern affirms God, because he affirms ultimacy in his concern. God is the fundamental symbol for what concerns us ultimately. Again it would be completely wrong to ask: So God is nothing but a symbol? Because the next question has to be: A symbol for what? And then the answer would be: For God! God is symbol for God. This means that in the notion of God we must distinguish two elements: the element of ultimacy, which is a matter of immediate experience and not symbolic in itself, and the element of concreteness, which is taken from our ordinary experience and symbolically applied to God. The man whose ultimate concern is a sacred tree has both the ultimacy of concern and the concreteness of the tree which symbolizes his relation to the ultimate. The man who adores Apollo is ultimately concerned, but not in an abstract way. His ultimate concern is symbolized in the divine figure of Apollo. The man who glorifies Jahweh, the God of the Old Testament, has both an ultimate concern and a concrete image of what concerns him ultimately. This is the meaning of the seemingly cryptic statement that God is the symbol of God. In this qualified sense God is the fundamental and universal content of faith.

It is obvious that such an understanding of the meaning of God makes the discussions about the existence or nonexistence of God meaningless. It is meaningless to question the ultimacy of an ultimate concern. This element in the idea of God is in itself certain. The symbolic expression of this element varies endlessly through the whole history of mankind. Here again it would be meaningless to ask whether one or another of the figures in which an ultimate concern is symbolized does "exist." If "existence" refers to something which can be found within the whole of reality, no divine being exists. The question is not this, but: which of the innumerable symbols of faith is most adequate to the meaning of faith? In other words, which symbol of ultimacy expresses the ultimate without idolatrous elements? This is the problem, and not the so-called "existence of God"—which is in itself an impossible combination of words. God as the ultimate in man's ultimate concern is more certain than any other certainty, even that of oneself. God as symbolized in a divine figure is a matter of daring faith, of courage and risk.

God is the basic symbol of faith, but not the only one. All the qualities we attribute to him, power, love, justice, are taken from finite experiences and applied symbolically to that which is beyond finitude and infinity. If faith calls God "almighty," it uses the human experience of power in order to symbolize the content of its infinite concern, but it does not describe a highest being who can do as he pleases. So it is with all the other qualities and with all the actions, past, present and future, which men attribute to God. They are symbols

taken from our daily experience, and not information about what God did once upon a time or will
do sometime in the future. Faith is not the belief in
such stories, but it is the acceptance of symbols that
express our ultimate concern in terms of divine
actions.

Another group of symbols of faith are manifestations of the divine in things and events, in persons
and communities, in words and documents. This
whole realm of sacred objects is a treasure of symbols. Holy things are not holy in themselves, but
they point beyond themselves to the source of all
holiness, that which is of ultimate concern.

3. Symbols and Myths

The symbols of faith do not appear in isolation.
They are united in "stories of the gods," which is
the meaning of the Greek word "mythos"—myth.
The gods are individualized figures, analogous to
human personalities, sexually differentiated, descend-
ing from each other, related to each other in love
and struggle, producing world and man, acting in
time and space. They participate in human greatness
and misery, in creative and destructive works. They
give to man cultural and religious traditions, and
defend these sacred rites. They help and threaten the
human race, especially some families, tribes or

nations. They appear in epiphanies and incarnations, establish sacred places, rites and persons, and thus create a cult. But they themselves are under the command and threat of a fate which is beyond everything that is. This is mythology as developed most impressively in ancient Greece. But many of these characteristics can be found in every mythology. Usually the mythological gods are not equals. There is a hierarchy, at the top of which is a ruling god, as in Greece; or a trinity of them, as in India; or a duality of them, as in Persia. There are savior-gods who mediate between the highest gods and man, sometimes sharing the suffering and death of man in spite of their essential immortality. This is the world of the myth, great and strange, always changing but fundamentally the same: man's ultimate concern symbolized in divine figures and actions. Myths are symbols of faith combined in stories about divine-human encounters.

Myths are always present in every act of faith, because the language of faith is the symbol. They are also attacked, criticized and transcended in each of the great religions of mankind. The reason for this criticism is the very nature of the myth. It uses material from our ordinary experience. It puts the stories of the gods into the framework of time and space although it belongs to the nature of the ultimate to be beyond time and space. Above all, it

divides the divine into several figures, removing ultimacy from each of them without removing their
claim to ultimacy. This inescapably leads to conflicts
of ultimate claims, able to destroy life, society and
consciousness.

The criticism of the myth first rejects the division of the divine and goes beyond it to one God,
although in different ways according to the different
types of religion. Even one God is an object of
mythological language, and if spoken about is drawn
into the framework of time and space. Even he loses
his ultimacy if made to be the content of concrete
concern. Consequently, the criticism of the myth
does not end with the rejection of the polytheistic
mythology.

Monotheism also falls under the criticism of the
myth. It needs, as one says today, "demythologization." This word has been used in connection with
the elaboration of the mythical elements in stories
and symbols of the Bible, both of the Old and the
New Testaments—stories like those of the Paradise,
of the fall of Adam, of the great Flood, of the
Exodus from Egypt, of the virgin birth of the
Messiah, of many of his miracles, of his resurrection
and ascension, of his expected return as the judge
of the universe. In short, all the stories in which
divine-human interactions are told are considered as
mythological in character, and objects of demythol-

ogization. What does this negative and artificial term mean? It must be accepted and supported if it points to the necessity of recognizing a symbol as a symbol and a myth as a myth. It must be attacked and rejected if it means the removal of symbols and myths altogether. Such an attempt is the third step in the criticism of the myth. It is an attempt which never can be successful, because symbol and myth are forms of the human consciousness which are always present. One can replace one myth by another, but one cannot remove the myth from man's spiritual life. For the myth is the combination of symbols of our ultimate concern.

A myth which is understood as a myth, but not removed or replaced, can be called a "broken myth." Christianity denies by its very nature any unbroken myth, because its presupposition is the first commandment: the affirmation of the ultimate as ultimate and the rejection of any kind of idolatry. All mythological elements in the Bible, and doctrine and liturgy should be recognized as mythological, but they should be maintained in their symbolic form and not be replaced by scientific substitutes. For there is no substitute for the use of symbols and myths: they are the language of faith.

The radical criticism of the myth is due to the fact that the primitive mythological consciousness resists the attempt to interpret the myth of myth.

It is afraid of every act of demythologization. It believes that the broken myth is deprived of its truth and of its convincing power. Those who live in an unbroken mythological world feel safe and certain. They resist, often fanatically, any attempt to introduce an element of uncertainty by "breaking the myth," namely, by making conscious its symbolic character. Such resistance is supported by authoritarian systems, religious or political, in order to give security to the people under their control and unchallenged power to those who exercise the control. The resistance against demythologization expresses itself in "literalism." The symbols and myths are understood in their immediate meaning. The material, taken from nature and history, is used in its proper sense. The character of the symbol to point beyond itself to something else is disregarded. Creation is taken as a magic act which happened once upon a time. The fall of Adam is localized on a special geographical point and attributed to a human individual. The virgin birth of the Messiah is understood in biological terms, resurrection and ascension as physical events, the second coming of the Christ as a telluric, or cosmic, catastrophe. The presupposition of such literalism is that God is a being, acting in time and space, dwelling in a special place, affecting the course of events and being affected by them like any other being in the universe. Literalism deprives God of his ultimacy and, religiously speaking, of his majesty. It draws him down to the level of that which is not ultimate, the finite and conditional. In the last analysis it is not rational criticism of the myth which is decisive but the inner religious criticism. Faith, if it takes its symbols literally, becomes idolatrous! It calls something ultimate which is less than ultimate. Faith, conscious of the symbolic character of its symbols, gives God the honor which is due him.

One should distinguish two stages of literalism, the natural and the reactive. The natural stage of literalism is that in which the mythical and the literal are indistinguishable. The primitive period of individuals and groups consists in the inability to separate the creations of symbolic imagination from the facts which can be verified through observation and experiment. This stage has a full right of its own and should not be disturbed, either in individuals or in groups, up to the moment when man's questioning mind breaks the natural acceptance of the mythological visions as literal. If, however, this moment has come, two ways are possible. The one is to replace the unbroken by the broken myth. It is the objectively demanded way, although it is impossible for many people who prefer the repression of their questions to the uncertainty which appears with the breaking of the myth. They are forced into the second stage of literalism, the conscious one, which is aware of the questions but represses them, half consciously, half unconsciously. The tool of repression is usually an acknowledged authority with sacred qualities like the Church or the Bible, to which one owes unconditional surrender. This stage is still justifiable, if the questioning power is very weak and can easily be answered. It is unjustifiable if a mature mind is broken in its personal center by political or psychological methods, split in its unity, and hurt in its integrity. The enemy of a critical theology is not natural literalism but conscious literalism with repression of and aggression toward autonomous thought.

Symbols of faith cannot be replaced by other symbols, such as artistic ones, and they cannot be removed by scientific criticism. They have a genuine standing in the human mind, just as science and art have. Their symbolic character is their truth and their power. Nothing less than symbols and myths can express our ultimate concern.

One more question arises, namely, whether myths are able to express every kind of ultimate concern. For example, Christian theologians argue that the word "myth" should be reserved for natural myths in which repetitive natural processes, such as the seasons, are understood in their ultimate meaning. They believe that if the world is seen as a historical process with beginning, end and center, as in Christianity and Judaism, the term "myth" should not be used. This would radically reduce the realm in which the term would be applicable. Myth could not be understood as the language of our ultimate concern, but only as a discarded idiom of this language. Yet history proves that there are not only natural myths but also historical myths. If the earth is seen as the battleground of two divine powers, as in ancient Persia, this is an historical myth. If the God of creation selects and guides a nation through history toward an end which transcends all history, this is an historical myth. If the Christ—a transcendent, divine being—appears in the fullness of time, lives, dies and is resurrected, this is an historical myth. Christianity is superior to those religions which are bound to a natural myth. But Christianity speaks the mythological language like every other religion. It is a broken myth, but it is a myth; otherwise Christianity would not be an expression of ultimate concern.

IV

⚝

TYPES OF FAITH

1. ELEMENTS OF FAITH AND THEIR DYNAMICS

Faith as the state of being ultimately concerned lives in many forms, subjectively and objectively. Every religious and cultural group and, to a certain degree, every individual is the bearer of a special experience and content of faith. The subjective state of the faithful changes in correlation to the change of the symbols of faith. In order to analyze the manifold expressions of faith, it is useful to distinguish some basic types and then to describe their dynamic interrelations. Types as such are static, standing alongside each other. But they also have a dynamic element. They claim ultimate validity for the special aspect of faith which they represent. This creates the tensions and struggles among the different types of faith within every religious community and among the great religions themselves.

Here it must be stated clearly that types are constructions of thought, and not things to be found in reality. There are no pure types in any realm of life. All real things participate in several types. But there are prevailing characteristics which determine a type and which must be elaborated in order to make the dynamics of life understandable. This is also true of the forms and expressions of faith. They show typical traits; but in every act of faith several traits are combined under the predominance of one of them.

For example, one can distinguish two main elements in every experience of the holy. One element is the presence of the holy here and now. It consecrates the place and the reality of its appearance. It grasps the mind with terrifying and fascinating power. It breaks into ordinary reality, shakes it and drives it beyond itself in an ecstatic way. It establishes rules according to which it can be approached. The holy must be present and felt as present in order to be experienced at all.

At the same time, the holy is the judgment over everything that is. It demands personal and social holiness in the sense of justice and love. Our ultimate concern represents what we essentially are and—therefore—ought to be. It stands as the law of our being, against us and for us. Holiness cannot be experienced without its power to command what we should be.

If we call the first element in the experience of the holy the holiness of being, the second element in the experience of the holy could be called the holiness of what ought to be. In an abbreviated way one could call the first form of faith its ontological type, and the second form its moral type. The dynamics of faith within and between the religions are largely determined by these two types, their interdependence and their conflicts. Their influence reaches into the most intimate cells of personal faith as well as into the movement of the great historical religions. They are omnipresent in every act of faith. But one of them is always predominant; for man is finite, and he can never unite all elements of truth in complete balance. On the other hand, he cannot rest on the awareness of his finitude, because faith is concerned with the ultimate and its adequate expression. Man's faith is inadequate if his whole existence is determined by something that is less than ultimate. Therefore, he must always try to break through the limits of his finitude and reach what never can be reached, the ultimate itself. Out of this tension the problem of faith and tolerance arises. A tolerance bound to relativism, to an attitude in which nothing ultimate is asked for, is negative and without content. It is doomed to swing toward its own opposite, an intolerant absolutism. Faith must unite the tolerance based on its relativity with the certainty based on the ultimacy of its concern. In all types of faith this problem is alive, but especially in the Protestant form of Christianity. From the power of self-criticism and from the courage to face one's own relativity come the greatness and danger of the Protestant faith. Here more than anywhere else the dynamics of faith become manifest and conscious: the infinite tension between the absoluteness of its claim and the relativity of its life.

2. Ontological Types of Faith

The holy is first of all experienced as present. It is here and now, and this means it encounters us in a thing, in a person, in an event. Faith sees in a concrete piece of reality the ultimate ground and meaning of all reality. No piece of reality is excluded from the possibility of becoming a bearer of the holy; and almost every kind of reality has actually been considered as holy by acts of faith in groups and individuals. Such a piece of reality has, as the traditional word says, "sacramental" character. This jar of water, this piece of bread, this cup of wine, this tree, this movement of the hands, of the knees, this building, this river, this color, this word, this book, this person is a bearer of the holy. In them faith experiences the content of its ultimate concern. They are not chosen arbitrarily but through visionary experiences of individuals. They are accepted by the collective reaction of groups, surrendered from generation to generation, changed, reduced, increased. They produce awe, fascination, adoration, idolatrous distortion, criticism, replacement by other bearers of the holy. This sacramental type of faith is the universal one. It is present in all religions. It is the daily bread of faith without which it becomes empty, abstract, and without significance for the life of individuals and groups.

Faith, in the sacramental type of religion, is not the belief that something *is* holy and other things are not. It is the state of being grasped by the holy through a special medium. The assertion that something has sacred character is meaningful only for the asserting faith. As a theoretical judgment claiming general validity, it is a meaningless combination of words. But in the correlation between the subject and the object of faith, it has meaning and truth. The outside observer can only state that there is a correlation of faith between the one who has faith and the sacramental object of his faith. But he cannot deny or affirm the validity of this correlation of faith. He can only state it as a fact. If a Protestant observes a Catholic praying before a picture of the Virgin, he remains observer, unable to state whether the faith of the observed is valid or not. If he is a Catholic he may join the observed in the same act of faith. There is no criterion by which faith can be judged from outside the correlation of faith. But something else can happen: The faithful can ask himself or be asked by someone else whether the medium through which he experiences ultimate concern expresses real ultimacy. This question is the dynamic force in the history of religion, revolutionizing the sacramental type of faith and driving faith beyond in different directions.

The presupposition of this question is the inadequacy of the finite—even the most sacred piece of reality—to express what is of ultimate concern. The human mind, however, forgets this inadequacy and identifies the sacred object with the ultimate itself. The sacramental object is taken as holy in itself. Its character as the bearer of the holy, pointing beyond itself, disappears in the act of faith. The act of faith is no longer directed toward the ultimate self, but toward that which represents the ultimate—the tree, the book, the building, the person. The transparence of faith is lost. It is the Protestant conviction that the Catholic doctrine of the "transubstantiation" of bread and wine in the Lord's Supper into the body and the blood of the Christ means just such a loss of the transparence of the divine and its identification with a segment of the encountered world. Faith experiences the presence of the holy, as embodied in the picture of the Christ, in the bread and wine of the Lord's Supper. Yet it is a doctrinal distortion of faith if the bread and the wine of the sacraments are considered as sacred objects effective in themselves and able to be preserved in a shrine. Nothing is sacred except in the correlation of faith. Even the saints are saints only because the source of all holiness is transparent through them.

The limits and dangers of the sacramental type of faith have in all periods of history driven mystics to the radical step of transcending in their faith every piece of reality as well as reality as a whole. They identified the ultimate with the ground or substance of everything—the one, the ineffable, the being above being. The interest of mystical faith is not to reject the concrete, sacramental ways of faith, but to go beyond them. Mystical faith is the end of a long way from the most concrete forms of faith to the point in which all concreteness disappears in the abyss of pure divinity. Mysticism is not irrational. Some of the greatest mystics in Europe and Asia were, at the same time, some of the greatest philosophers, outstanding in clarity, consistency and rationality. But they realized that the true content of faith in an ultimate concern can neither be identified with a piece of reality, as sacramental faith desires, nor be expressed in terms of a rational system. It is a matter of ecstatic experience, and one can only speak of the ultimate in a language which at the same time denies the possibility of speaking about it. This is the only way in which mystical faith can express itself. But one may ask: Is there anything to express at all if the content of mystical faith transcends anything expressible? Is not faith based on the experience of the presence of the holy? How is such an experience possible if the ultimate is that which transcends all possible experience? The answer given by the mystics is that there is a place where the ultimate is present within the finite world, namely, the depth of the human soul. This depth is the point of contact between the finite and the infinite. In order to go into it, man must empty himself of all the finite contents of his ordinary life; he must surrender all preliminary concerns for the sake of the ultimate concern. He must go beyond the pieces of reality in which sacramental faith experiences the ultimate. He must transcend the division of existence, even the deepest and most universal of all divisions, that between subject and object. The ultimate is beyond this division, and he who wants to reach the ultimate must overcome this division in himself by meditation, contemplation and ecstasy. Faith, within this movement of the soul, is in a state of oscillation between having and not having the content of ultimate concern. It moves in degrees of approximation, in relapses and sudden fulfillments. The mystical faith does not despise or reject the sacramental faith. It goes beyond it to that which is present in every act of sacramental faith, yet hidden under the concrete objects in which it is embodied. Theologians sometimes have contrasted faith and mystical experience. They say the distance between faith and the ultimate can never be bridged. Mysticism tries to merge the mind with the content of its unconditional concern, with the ground of being and meaning. But this contrast has only limited validity. The mystic is aware of the infinite distance between the infinite and the finite, and accepts a life of preliminary stages of union with the infinite, interrupted only rarely, and perhaps never, in this life by the final ecstasy. And the faithful can have faith only if he is grasped by the content of his ultimate concern. Like sacramentalism, mysticism is a type of faith; and there is a mystical as well as a sacramental element in every type of faith.

This is true even of the humanist kind of the ontological type of faith. A consideration of this kind of faith is especially important, because humanism is often identified with unbelief and contrasted with faith. This is possible only if faith is defined as belief in the existence and actions of divine beings. However, if faith is understood as the state of being ultimately concerned about the ultimate, humanism implies faith. Humanism is the attitude which makes man the measure of his own spiritual life, in art and philosophy, in science and politics, in social relations and personal ethics. For humanism the divine is manifest in the human; the ultimate concern of man is man. All this, of course, refers to man in his essence: the true man, the man of the idea, not the actual man, nor the man in estrangement from his true nature. If, in this sense, the humanist says that his ultimate concern is man, he sees man as the ultimate in finite reality, just as sacramental faith sees the ultimate in a piece of reality or as mystical faith finds in the depth of man the place of the infinite. The difference is that the sacramental and mystical types transcend the limits of humanity and try to reach the ultimate itself beyond man and his world, while the humanist remains within these limits. For this reason the humanist faith is called "secular," in contrast to the two types of faith which are called "religious." Secular means belonging to the ordinary process of events, not going beside it or beyond it into a sanctuary. In Latin and some derived languages one speaks of profanity in the sense of "being before the doors of the temple." Profane in this sense is the same as secular. Often people say that they are secular, that they live outside the doors of the temple, and consequently that they are without faith! But if one asks them whether they are without an ultimate concern, without something which they take as unconditionally serious, they would strongly deny this. And in denying that they are without an ultimate concern, they affirm that they are in a state of faith. They represent the humanist type of faith which itself is full of varieties; the fact that they are secular does not exclude them from the community of the faithful.

It is an almost infinite task to describe the manifold forms in which the humanist type of faith has expressed itself and is alive in large sections of the Western world and in the Asiatic cultures. If we apply to it the distinction we have applied to the religious types of faith, the distinction between the ontological and the moral type, we can say that the ontological type of secular faith is romantic-conservative, the moral type is progressive-utopian. The word "romantic," in this context, points to the experience of the infinite in the finite, as it is given in nature and history. The word "conservative" in connection with romantic emphasizes the experience of the presence of the ultimate in the existing forms of nature and history. If a man sees the holy in the flower as it grows, in the animal as it moves, in man as he represents a unique individuality, in a special nation, a special culture, a special social system, he is romantic-conservative. For him the given is holy and is the content of his ultimate concern.

The analogy of this kind of faith to the sacramental faith is obvious. The romantic-conservative type of humanist faith is secularized sacramental faith: the divine is given here and now. All cultural and political conservatism is derived from this type of secular faith. It is faith, but it hides the dimension of the ultimate which it presupposes. Its weakness and its danger is that it may become empty. History has shown this weakness and final emptiness of all merely secular cultures. It has turned them back again and again to the religious forms of faith from which they came.

3. MORAL TYPES OF FAITH

The moral types of faith are characterized by the idea of the law. God is the God who has given the law as a gift and as a command. He can be approached only by those who obey the law. There are, of course, laws in the sacramental and mystical types of faith, and no one can reach the ultimate without fulfilling these laws. But there is an important difference between the laws in the two types of faith. The law in the ontological types demands subjection to ritual methods or ascetic practices. The law in the moral type demands moral obedience. The difference, certainly, is not absolute. For the ritual law includes moral conditions and the eth-

ical law includes ontological conditions. But the difference is sufficient to make understandable the rise
of the various great religions. They follow the one
or the other type.

One can distinguish the juristic, the conventional and the ethical in the moral types of faith. The
juristic type is most strongly developed in Talmudic
Judaism and in Islam; the conventional type is most
prominent in Confucianist China; the ethical type is
represented by the Jewish prophets.

The faith of a Moslem is faith in the revelation
given by Mohammed, and this revelation is his ultimate concern. The revelations mediated by Mohammed are largely ritual and social laws. The ritual laws
point to the sacramental stage out of which all religions and cultures have arisen. The social laws transcend the ritual element and produce a holiness of
"what ought to be." These laws permeate the whole
life (as they do in orthodox Judaism). Their source
is a matter of ultimate concern, the prophet; their
content is identical with his commands. The law is
always felt as both a gift and a command. Under the
protection of the law, life is possible and satisfying.
This is true of the average adherent of Islam and it
is true of those who develop on this basis a secular
humanism, nourished largely by Greek sources. If
somebody who knows the religious attitude of the
Islamic nations said that this is faith in Mohammed,

conflicting with faith in Christ, one has to answer that it is not the faith in Mohammed as *the* prophet which is decisive, but the faith in an order which is consecrated and determines the daily life of most people. The question of faith is not Moses or Jesus or Mohammed; the question is: Who expresses most adequately one's ultimate concern? The conflict between religions is not a conflict between forms of belief, but it is a conflict between expressions of our ultimate concern. The question is whether the manifestation of the divine in the juristic realm is its ultimate manifestation. All decisions of faith are existential, not theoretical, decisions.

This is also true of a system of conventional rules as collected and formulated by Confucius. This system has often been called unreligious and a complete lack of faith has been attributed to the Chinese way of life, in so far as it is determined by Confucius. There is faith in Confucianism, not only in the worship of the ancestors (which is a sacramental element) but also in the unconditional character of the commands. And in the background is the vision of the law of the universe, of which the laws of state and society are a manifestation. Yet in spite of these religious elements in Confucianism, its basic character is secular. This accounts for two world historical facts. It is the negative condition for the influence of the sacramental and mystical religions of Buddhism

and Taoism in China in their popular as well as their
sophisticated forms. And it is the positive condition
for the easy victory of the secular faith of com-
munism which also belongs to the moral types of
humanist faith.

The third and most influential form of the moral
types of religious faith is Old Testament Judaism.
Like every faith, it has a broad sacramental basis: the
idea of the elected nation, the covenant between
God and the nation, and the ritual law in all its rich-
ness and abundance of sacramental activities. But
the experience of the holiness of being has never
overwhelmed the experience of the holiness of
"ought to be." For the Jewish prophets, and all
their followers among priests and rabbis and theologians, obedience to the law of justice is the way of
reaching God. The divine law is of ultimate concern
in old and new Judaism. It is the central content of
faith. It gives rules for a continuous actualization of
the ultimate concern within the preliminary concerns of the daily life. The ultimate shall always be
present and remembered even in the smallest activities of the ordinary life. On the other hand, all this
is worth nothing if it is not united with obedience
to the moral law, the law of justice and righteous-
ness. The final criterion for the relation of man
to God is subjection to the law of justice. It is
the greatness of Old Testament prophetism that it

undercut again and again the desire of the people and, even more, of its leaders to rely on the sacramental element of the law and to neglect the moral element—the "ought to be" as the criterion of the "being." The world historical mission of the Jewish faith is to judge the sacramental self-certainty in Judaism itself, as well as in all other religions, and to pronounce an ultimate concern which denies any claim for ultimacy that does not include the demand of justice.

The influence of Judaism is visible not only in Christianity and Islam but also in the progressive-utopian type of humanist faith found in the Western world. Ancient humanism is certainly aware of the "ought to be." Greek mythology and tragic poetry, Greek wisdom and philosophy, Roman law and the political humanism of the Roman Stoics show the emphasis on the "ought to be." But the ontological type remained predominant in all ancient history. The victory of mysticism in Greek philosophy and of the mystery religions in the Roman Empire, the lack of progressive and utopian thinking in the sphere of antiquity prove it.

Modern humanism, especially since the eighteenth century, rests on a Christian foundation and includes the dominant emphasis on the "ought to be," as elaborated by the Jewish prophets. Consequently, it shows from its beginnings strong progressive and utopian elements. It starts with the criticism of the feudal order and its sacramental foundations. It demands justice; first for the peasants, then for the bourgeois society, then for the proletarian masses. The faith of the fighters for enlightenment since the eighteenth century is humanist faith of the moral type. They fought for freedom from sacramentally consecrated bondage and for justice for every human being. Their faith was humanist faith, expressing itself in secular more than in religious terms. It was faith and not rational calculation, although they believed in the superior power of a reason united with justice and truth. The dynamics of their humanist faith changed the face of the earth, first in the West, then also in the East. It is this humanist faith of the moral type which was taken over by the revolutionary movement of the proletarian masses in the nineteenth and twentieth centuries. Its dynamic is visible every day in our present period. As for every faith, the utopian form of the humanist faith is a state of ultimate concern. This gives it its tremendous power for good and evil. In view of this (and the preceding) analysis of humanist faith, it is almost ridiculous to speak of the loss of faith in the Western secular world. It has a secular faith, and this has pushed the different forms of religion into a defensive position; but it is faith and not "unbelief." It is a state of ultimate concern and total devotion to this concern.

4. THE UNITY OF THE TYPES OF FAITH

In the experience of the holy, the ontological and the moral element are essentially united, while in the life of faith they diverge and are driven to conflicts and mutual destruction. Nevertheless, the essential unity cannot be completely dissolved: there are always elements of the one type within the other, as previously indicated. In the sacramental type of faith the ritual law is omnipresent, demanding purification, preparation, subjection to the liturgical rules, and ethical fitness. On the other hand, we have seen how many ritual elements are present in the religions of the law—the moral type of faith. This is true even of the humanist faith, where progressive and utopian elements can be found in the romantic-conservative type, while the progressive-utopian type is based on given traditions from which it criticizes the present situation and drives beyond it. The mutual participation of the types of faith in each other makes each of them complex, dynamic and self-transcending.

The history of faith, which is more embracing than the history of religion, is a movement of divergence and convergence of the different types of faith. This is true of the act of faith as well as of the content of faith. The expressions of man's ultimate concern, understood subjectively as well as objectively, are not a chaos of unlimited varieties. They are representations of basic attitudes which have developed in the history of faith and are consequences of the nature of faith. Therefore, it is possible to understand and describe their movements against and toward each other and perhaps to show a point at which their reunion is reached in principle. It is obvious that the attempt to do this is dependent on the ultimate concern of the person making the attempt. If he happens to be a Christian theologian of the Protestant type, he will see in Christianity—and especially Protestant Christianity—the aim toward which the dynamics of faith are driving. This cannot be avoided, because faith is a matter of personal concern. At the same time, he who makes the attempt must give objective reasons for his decision. "Objective" means in this case: derived from the nature of faith which is the same in all types of faith—if the term "faith" is to be used at all.

Roman Catholicism rightly has called itself a system which unites the most divergent elements of man's religious and cultural life. Its sources are the Old Testament, which itself combines the sacramental and the moral type, Hellenistic mystery religions, individual mysticism, classical Greek humanism, and the scientific methods of later antiquity. Above all, it is based directly on the New Testament, which in itself includes a variety of types and represents a union of ethical and mystical elements. A conspicuous example is Paul's description of the Spirit. Faith, in the New Testament, is the state of being grasped by the divine Spirit. As *Spirit* it is the presence of the divine power in the human mind; as *holy* Spirit it is the Spirit of love, justice and truth. I would not hesitate to call this description of the Spirit the answer to the question and the fulfillment of the dynamics which drive the history of faith. But such an answer is not a place to rest upon. It must be given again and again on the basis of new experiences, and under changing conditions. Only if this is done does it remain an answer and a possible fulfillment. Neither Catholicism nor fundamentalism is aware of this necessity. Therefore, both have lost elements of the original union and have fallen under the predominance of one or the other side. This is the point where the Protestant protest has arisen before, during and after the Reformation of the sixteenth century. This is the point where the Protestant protest must always arise in the name of the ultimacy of the ultimate.

The general criticism of the Roman Church by

all Protestant groups was the exclusion of the prophetic self-criticism by the authoritarian system of the Church and the growth of the sacramental elements of faith over the moral-personal ones. The first point made a change of the second within the Church impossible, and so a break was unavoidable. But the break brought about a loss of Roman sacramentalism and the uniting authority based on them. In consequence of this loss, Protestantism became more and more a representative of the moral type of ultimate concern. In this way it lost not only the large number of ritual traditions in the Catholic churches but also a full understanding of the presence of the holy in sacramental and mystical experiences. The Pauline experience of the Spirit as the unity of all types of faith was largely lost in both Catholicism and Protestantism. It is the attempt of the present description of faith to point, in contemporary terminology, to the reality of Paul's understanding of the Spirit as the unity of the ecstatic and the person, of the sacramental and the moral, of the mystical and the rational. Only if Christianity is able to regain in real experience this unity of the divergent types of faith can it express its claim to answer the questions and to fulfill the dynamics of the history of faith in past and future.

V

✠

THE TRUTH OF FAITH

1. FAITH AND REASON

We have pointed to the limitless variety of symbols and to the many contrasting types of faith. This seems to imply a complete denial of the claim these symbols and types have to truth. Therefore, we must now discuss the question whether, and in what sense, faith can be judged in terms of truth.

The most usual way in which this problem has been discussed is to contrast faith with reason, and to ask whether they exclude each other or whether they can be united in a reasonable faith. If the latter is possible, how are the elements of rationality and of faith related to each other? Obviously, if the meaning of faith is misunderstood in the ways we have indicated before, faith and reason exclude each other. If, however, faith is understood as the state of being ultimately concerned, no conflict need exist.

But this answer is insufficient, because man's spiritual life is a unity and does not admit elements alongside each other. All spiritual elements of man, in spite of their distinct character, are within each other. This is true also of faith and reason. Therefore, it is not enough to assert that the state of being ultimately concerned is in no conflict with the rational structure of the human mind. One also must show their actual relationship, namely, the way in which they lie within each other. In which sense, one must ask first, is the word "reason" used when confronted with faith? Is it meant, as is often the case today, in the sense of scientific method, logical strictness and technical calculation? Or is it used, as in most periods of Western culture, in the sense of the source of meaning, of structure, of norms and principles? In the first case, reason gives the tools for recognizing and controlling reality, and faith gives the direction in which this control may be exercised. One could call this kind of reason technical reason, providing for means but not for ends. Reason in this sense concerns the daily life of everybody and is the power which determines the technical civilization of our time. In the second case, reason is identical with the humanity of man in contrast to all other beings. It is the basis of language, of freedom, of creativity.

It is involved in the search for knowledge, the experience of art, the actualization of moral commands; it makes a centered personal life and a participation in community possible. If faith were the opposite of reason, it would tend to dehumanize man. This consequence has been drawn, theoretically and practically, in religious and political authoritarian systems. A faith which destroys reason destroys itself and the humanity of man. For only a being who has the structure of reason is able to be ultimately concerned, to distinguish ultimate and preliminary concerns, to understand the unconditional commands of the ethical imperative, and to be aware of the presence of the holy. All this is valid only if the second meaning of reason is presupposed: reason as the meaningful structure of mind and reality; and not the first meaning: reason as a technical tool.

Reason is the precondition of faith; faith is the act in which reason reaches ecstatically beyond itself. This is the opposite side of their being within each other. Man's reason is finite; it moves within finite relations when dealing with the universe and with man himself. All cultural activities in which man perceives his world and those in which he shapes his world have this character of finitude. Therefore, they are not matters of infinite concern. But reason is not bound to its own finitude. It is aware of it and, in so doing, rises above it. Man experiences a belonging to the infinite which, however, is neither a part of himself nor something in his power. It must grasp him, and if it does, it is a matter of infinite concern. Man is finite, man's reason lives in preliminary concerns; but man is also aware of his potential infinity, and this awareness appears as his ultimate concern, as faith. If reason is grasped by an ultimate concern, it is driven beyond itself; but it does not cease to be reason, finite reason. The ecstatic experience of an ultimate concern does not destroy the structure of reason. Ecstasy is fulfilled, not denied, rationality. Reason can be fulfilled only if it is driven beyond the limits of its finitude, and experiences the presence of the ultimate, the holy. Without such an experience reason exhausts itself and its finite contents. Finally, it becomes filled with irrational or demonic contents and is destroyed by them. The road leads from reason fulfilled in faith through reason without faith to reason filled with demonic-destructive faith. The second stage is only a point of transition, since there is no vacuum in the spiritual life, as there is none in nature. Reason is the presupposition of faith, and faith is the fulfillment of reason. Faith as the state of ultimate concern is reason in ecstasy. There is no conflict between the nature of faith and the nature of reason; they are within each other.

On this point theology will ask several questions. It will ask whether the nature of faith is not distorted under the conditions of human existence, for example, if demonic-destructive forces get hold of it—as indicated before. And theology will ask whether the nature of reason is not distorted with man's estrangement from himself. Finally, it will ask whether the unity of faith and reason and the true nature of both of them must not be re-established by what religion calls "revelation." And—theology will continue—if this is the case, is reason in its distorted stage not obliged to subject itself to revelation and is not this subjection to the contents of revelation the true sense of the term "faith"? The answer to these questions, asked by theology, is the matter of a whole theology itself. It cannot be given in the present book except in a few basic statements.

First, it must be acknowledged that man is in a state of estrangement from his true nature. Thus the use of his reason and the character of his faith are not what they essentially are and, therefore, ought to be. This leads to actual conflicts between a distorted use of reason and an idolatrous faith. The solution we gave with respect to the true nature of faith and the true nature of reason cannot be applied without this fundamental qualification to the actual life of faith and reason under the conditions of human existence.

The consequence of this qualification is that the

estrangement of faith and of reason in themselves and in their mutual relationship must be overcome and their true nature and relation must be established within actual life. The experience in which this happens is a revelatory experience. The term "revelation" has been misused so much that it is difficult to use it at all, even more so than the term "reason." Revelation is popularly understood as a divine information about divine matters, given to prophets and apostles and dictated by the divine Spirit to the writers of the Bible, or the Koran, or other sacred books. Acceptance of such divine informations, however absurd and irrational they may be, is then called faith. Every word of the present discussion contradicts this distortion of the meaning of revelation. Revelation is first of all the experience in which an ultimate concern grasps the human mind and creates a community in which this concern expresses itself in symbols of action, imagination and thought. Wherever such a revelatory experience occurs, both faith and reason are renewed. Their internal and mutual conflicts are conquered, and estrangement is replaced by reconciliation. This is what revelation means, or should mean. It is an event in which the ultimate becomes manifest in an ultimate concern, shaking and transforming the given situation in religion and culture. In such an experience no conflict between faith and reason is possible; for it is man's total structure as a rational being which is grasped and changed by the revelatory manifestation of an ultimate concern. But revelation is relevation to man in his state of corrupted faith and corrupted rationality. And the corruption, although broken in its final power, is conquered but not removed. It enters the new revelatory experience as it had entered the old ones. It makes faith idolatrous, confusing the bearer and the manifestations of the ultimate with the ultimate itself. It deprives reason of its ecstatic power, of its tendency to transcend itself in the direction of the ultimate. In consequence of this dual distortion, it distorts the relation of faith and reason, reducing faith to a preliminary concern which interferes with the preliminary concerns of reason, and elevates reason to ultimacy in spite of its essential finitude. Out of this double corruption there arise new conflicts between faith and reason and with them the quest for a new and superior revelation. The history of faith is a permanent fight with the corruption of faith, and the conflict with reason is one of its most conspicuous symptoms. The decisive battles in this fight are the great revelatory events, and the victorious battle would be a final revelation in which the distortion of faith and reason is definitely overcome. Christianity claims to be based on this revelation. Its claim is exposed to the continuous pragmatic test of history.

2. THE TRUTH OF FAITH AND SCIENTIFIC TRUTH

There is no conflict between faith in its true nature and reason in its true nature. This includes the assertion that there is no essential conflict between faith and the cognitive function of reason. Cognition in all its forms was always considered as that function of man's reason which comes most easily into conflict with faith. This was especially so when faith was defined as a lower form of knowledge and was accepted because the divine authority guaranteed its truth. We have rejected this distortion of the meaning of faith, and in doing so have removed one of the most frequent causes for the conflicts between faith and knowledge. But we must show beyond this the concrete relation of faith to the several forms of cognitive reason: the scientific, the historical and the philosophical. The truth of faith is different from the meaning of truth in each of these ways of knowledge. Nevertheless, it is truth they all try to reach, truth in the sense of the "really real" received adequately by the cognitive function of the human mind. Error takes place if man's cognitive endeavor misses the really real and takes that which is only seemingly real for real; or if it hits the really real but expresses it in a distorted way. Often it is difficult to say whether the real is missed or whether its expression is inadequate, because the two forms of error are interdependent. In any case, where there is the attempt to know, there is truth or error or one of the many degrees of transition between truth and error. In faith man's cognitive function is at work. Therefore, we must ask what the meaning of truth in faith is, what its criteria are, and how it is related to other forms of truth with other kinds of criteria.

Science tries to describe and to explain the structures and relations in the universe, in so far as they can be tested by experiment and calculated in quantitative terms. The truth of a scientific statement is the adequacy of the description of the structural laws which determine reality, and it is the verification of this description by experimental repetitions. Every scientific truth is preliminary and subject to changes both in grasping reality and in expressing it adequately. This element of uncertainty does not diminish the truth value of a tested and verified scientific assertion. It only prevents scientific dogmatism and absolutism.

Therefore, it is a very poor method of defending the truth of faith against the truth of science, if theologians point to the preliminary character of every scientific statement in order to provide a place of retreat for the truth of faith. If tomorrow scientific progress reduced the sphere of uncertainty, faith would have to continue its retreat—an undignified and unnecessary procedure, for scientific truth and the truth of faith do not belong to the same dimension of meaning. Science has no right and no power to interfere with faith and faith has no power to interfere with science. One dimension of meaning is not able to interfere with another dimension.

If this is understood, the previous conflicts between faith and science appear in a quite different light. The conflict was actually not between faith and science but between a faith and a science each of which was not aware of its own valid dimension. When the representatives of faith impeded the beginning of modern astronomy they were not aware that the Christian symbols, although using the Aristotelian-Ptolemaic astronomy, were not tied up with this astronomy. Only if the symbols of "God in heaven" and "man on earth" and "demons below the earth" are taken as descriptions of places, populated by divine or demonic beings, can modern astronomy conflict with the Christian faith. On the other hand, if representatives of modern physics reduce the whole of reality to the mechanical movement of the smallest particles of matter, denying the really real quality of life and mind, they express a faith, objectively as well as subjectively. Subjectively science is their ultimate concern—and they are ready to sacrifice everything, including their lives, for this ultimate. Objectively, they create a monstrous symbol of this concern, namely, a universe in which everything, including their own scientific passion, is swallowed by a meaningless mechanism. In opposing this symbol of faith Christian faith is right.

Science can conflict only with science, and faith only with faith; science which remains science cannot conflict with faith which remains faith. This is true also of other spheres of scientific research, such as biology and psychology. The famous struggle between the theory of evolution and the theology of some Christian groups was not a struggle between science and faith, but between a science whose faith deprived man of his humanity and a faith whose expression was distorted by Biblical literalism. It is obvious that a theology which interprets the Biblical story of creation as a scientific description of an event which happened once upon a time interferes with the methodologically controlled scientific work; and that a theory of evolution which interprets man's descendance from older forms of life in a way that removes the infinite, qualitative difference between man and animal is faith and not science.

The same consideration must be given to present and future conflicts between faith and contemporary psychology. Modern psychology is afraid of the concept of soul because it seems to establish a reality which is unapproachable by scientific methods and may interfere with their results. This fear is not unfounded; psychology should not accept any concept which is not produced by its own scientific work. Its function is to describe man's processes as adequately as possible, and to be open to replacement of these descriptions at any time. This is true of the modern concepts of ego, superego, self, personality, unconsciousness, mind, as well as of the traditional concepts of soul, spirit, will, etc. Methodological psychology is subject to scientific verification, as is every other scientific endeavor. All its concepts and definitions, even those most validated, are preliminary.

When faith speaks of the ultimate dimension in which man lives, and in which he can win or lose his soul, or of the ultimate meaning of his existence, it is not interfering at all with the scientific rejection of the concept of the soul. A psychology without soul cannot deny this nor can a psychology with soul confirm it. The truth of man's eternal meaning lies in a dimension other than the truth of adequate psychological concepts. Contemporary analytic or depth psychology has in many instances conflicted with pre-theological and theological expressions of faith. It is, however, not difficult in the statements of depth psychology to distinguish the more or less verified observations and hypotheses from assertions about man's nature and destiny which are clearly expressions of faith. The naturalistic elements which Freud carried from the nineteenth into the twentieth century, his basic puritanism with respect to love, his pessimism about culture, and his reduction of religion to ideological projection are all expressions of faith and not the result of scientific analysis. There is no reason to deny to a scholar who deals with man and his predicament the right to introduce elements of faith. But if he attacks other forms of faith in the name of scientific psychology, as Freud and many of his followers do, he is confusing dimensions. In this case those who represent another kind of faith are justified in resisting these attacks. It is not always easy to distinguish the element of faith from the element of scientific hypothesis in a psychological assertion, but it is possible and often necessary.

The distinction between the truth of faith and the truth of science leads to a warning, directed to theologians, not to use recent scientific discoveries to confirm the truth of faith. Microphysics have undercut some scientific hypotheses concerning the calculability of the universe. The theory of quantum and the principle of indeterminacy have had this effect. Immediately religious writers use these insights for the confirmation of their own ideas of human freedom, divine creativity, and miracles. But there is no justification for such a procedure at all, neither from the point of view of physics nor from the point of view of religion. The physical theories referred to have no direct relation to the infinitely complex phenomenon of human freedom, and the emission of power in quantums has no direct relation to the meaning of miracles. Theology, in using physical theories in this way, confuses the dimension of science with the dimension of faith. The truth of faith cannot be confirmed by latest physical or biological or psychological discoveries—as it cannot be denied by them.

3. The Truth of Faith and Historical Truth

Historical truth has a character quite different from that of scientific truth. History reports unique events, not repetitious processes which can be tested again and again. Historical events are not subject to experiment. The only analogy in history to a physical experiment is the comparison of documents. If documents of an independent origin agree, a historical assertion is verified within its own limits. But history does not only tell a series of facts. It also tries to understand these facts in their origins, their relations, their meaning. History describes, explains and understands. And understanding presupposes participation. This is the difference between historical and scientific truth. In historical truth the interpreting subject is involved; in scientific truth it is detached. Since the truth of faith means total

involvement, historical truth has often been com-
pared with the truth of faith. A complete depen-
dence of the historical truth on the truth of faith has
been derived from such an identification. In this way
it has been asserted that faith can guarantee the
truth of a questionable historical statement. But he
who makes such assertions forgets that in a genuine
historical work detached and controlled observation
is as much used as in the observation of physical
or biological processes. Historical truth is first of
all factual truth; in this it is distinguished from
the poetic truth of epics or from the mythical truth
of legend. This difference is decisive for the relation
of the truth of faith to the truth of history. Faith
cannot guarantee factual truth. But faith can and
must interpret the meaning of facts from the point
of view of man's ultimate concern. In doing so
it transfers historical truth into the dimension of
the truth of faith.

This problem has come into the foreground of
much popular and theological thought since historical research has discovered the literary character of
the Biblical writings. It has shown that in their nar-
rative parts of the Old and the New Testament com-
bine historical, legendary and mythological elements
and that in many cases it is impossible to separate
these elements from each other with any degree of
probability. Historical research has made it obvious

that there is no way to get at the historical events which have produced the Biblical picture of Jesus who is called the Christ with more than a degree of probability. Similar research in the historical character of the holy writings and the legendary traditions of non-Christian religions has discovered the same situation. The truth of faith cannot be made dependent on the historical truth of the stories and legends in which faith has expressed itself. It is a disastrous distortion of the meaning of faith to identify it with the belief in the historical validity of the Biblical stories. This, however, happens on high as well as on low levels of sophistication. People say that others or they themselves are without Christian faith, because they do not believe that the New Testament miracle stories are reliably documented. Certainly they are not, and the search for the degree of probability or improbability of a Biblical story has to be made with all the tools of a solid philological and historical method. It is not a matter of faith to decide if the presently used edition of the Moslemic Koran is identical with the original text, although this is the fervent belief of most of the adherents of Mohammed. It is not a matter of faith to decide that large parts of the Pentateuch are priestly wisdom of the period after the Babylonic exile, or that the Book of Genesis contains more myths and sacred legend than actual history. It is not a matter of faith to decide whether or not the expectation of the final catastrophe of the universe as envisaged in the late books of the Old and in the New Testament originated in the Persian religion. It is not a matter of faith to decide how much legendary, mythological and historical material is amalgamated in the stories about the birth and the resurrection of the Christ. It is not a matter of faith to decide which version of the reports about the early days of the Church has the greatest probability. All these questions must be decided, in terms of more or less probability, by historical research. They are questions of historical truth, not of the truth of faith. Faith can say that something of ultimate concern has happened in history because the question of the ultimate in being and meaning is involved. Faith can say that the Old Testament law which is given as the law of Moses has unconditional validity for those who are grasped by it, no matter how much or how little can be traced to a historical figure of that name. Faith can say that the reality which is manifest in the New Testament picture of Jesus as the Christ has saving power for those who are grasped by it, no matter how much or how little can be traced to the historical figure who is called Jesus of Nazareth. Faith can ascertain its own foundation, the Mosaic law, or Jesus as the Christ, Mohammed the prophet, or Buddha the illuminated. But faith cannot ascertain the historical conditions which made it possible for these men to become matters of ultimate concern for large sections of humanity. Faith includes certitude about its own foundation—for example, an event in history which has transformed history—for the faithful. But faith does not include historical knowledge about the way in which this event took place. Therefore, faith cannot be shaken by historical research even if its results are critical of the traditions in which the event is reported. This independence of historical truth is one of the most important consequences of the understanding of faith as the state of ultimate concern. It liberates the faithful from a burden they cannot carry after the demands of scholarly honesty have shaped their conscience. If such honesty were in a necessary conflict with what has been called the "obedience of faith," God would be seen as split in himself, as having demonic traits; and the concern about it would not be ultimate concern, but the conflict of two limited concerns. Such faith, in the last analysis, is idolatrous.

4. The Truth of Faith and Philosophical Truth

Neither scientific nor historical truth can affirm or negate the truth of faith. The truth of faith can neither affirm nor negate scientific or historical truth. Then the question arises whether philosophical truth has the same relation to the truth of faith or whether the relation is more complex. This, indeed, is the case. What is more, the complexity of the relation between philosophical truth and the truth of faith makes the relation of scientific and historical truth more complex than it appeared in the preceding analysis. This is the reason for the innumerable discussions about the relationship of faith and philosophy and for the popular opinion that philosophy is the enemy and destroyer of faith. Even theologians who have used a philosophical concept in order to express the faith of a religious community have been accused of betraying the faith.

The difficulty of every discussion concerning philosophy as such is the fact that every definition of philosophy is an expression of the point of view of the philosopher who gives the definition. Nevertheless, there is a kind of pre-philosophical agreement about the meaning of philosophy, and the only thing one can do in a discussion like the present one is to use this prephilosophical notion of what philosophy is. In this sense philosophy is the attempt to answer the most general questions about the nature of reality and human existence. Most general are those questions which do not ask about the nature of a specific sphere of reality (as the physical or the historical realms) but about the nature of reality, which is effective in all realms. Philosophy tries to find the universal categories in which being is experienced.

If such a notion of philosophy is presupposed, the relation of philosophical truth to the truth of faith can be determined. Philosophical truth is truth about the structure of being; the truth of faith is truth about one's ultimate concern. Up to this point the relation seems to be very similar to that between the truth of faith and scientific truth. But the difference is that there is a point of identity between the ultimate of the philosophical question and the ultimate of the religious concern. In both cases ultimate reality is sought and expressed—conceptually in philosophy, symbolically in religion. Philosophical truth consists in true concepts concerning the ultimate; the truth of faith consists in true symbols concerning the ultimate. The relation between these two is the problem with which we have to deal.

The question will certainly be raised: Why does philosophy use concepts and why does faith use symbols if both try to express the same ultimate? The answer, of course, is that the relation to the ultimate is not the same in each case. The philosophical relation is in principle a detached description of the basic structure in which the ultimate manifests itself. The relation of faith is in principle an involved expression of concern about the meaning of the ultimate for the faithful. The difference is obvious and fundamental. But it is, as the phrase "in principle" indicates, a difference which is not maintained in the actual life of philosophy and of faith. It cannot be maintained, because the philosopher is a human being with an ultimate concern, hidden or open. And the faithful one is a human being with the power of thought and the need for conceptual understanding. This is not only a biographical fact. It has consequences for the life of philosophy in the philosopher and for the life of faith in the faithful.

An analysis of philosophical systems, essays or fragments of all kinds shows that the direction in which the philosopher asks the question and the preference he gives to special types of answers is determined by cognitive consideration and by a state of ultimate concern. The historically most significant philosophies show not only the greatest power of thought but the most passionate concern about the meaning of the ultimate whose manifestations they describe. One needs only to be reminded of the Indian and Greek philosophers, almost without exception, and the modern philosophers from Leibnitz and Spinoza to Kant and Hegel. If it seems that the positivistic line of philosophers from Locke and Hume to present-day logical positivism is an exception to this rule, one must consider that the task to which these philosophers restricted themselves were special problems of the doctrine of knowledge and, in our time especially, analyses of the linguistic tools of scientific knowledge. This certainly is a justified and very important endeavor, but is not philosophy in the traditional sense.

Philosophy, in its genuine meaning, is carried on by people in whom the passion of an ultimate concern is united with a clear and detached observation of the way ultimate reality manifests itself in the processes of the universe. It is this element of ultimate concern behind philosophical ideas which supplies the truth of faith in them. Their vision of the universe and of man's predicament within it unites faith and conceptual work. Philosophy is not only the mother's womb out of which science and history have come, it is also an ever-present element in actual scientific and historical work. The frame of reference within which the great physicists have seen and are seeing the universe of their inquiries is philosophical, even if their actual inquiries verify it. In no case is it a result of their discoveries. It is always a vision of the totality of being which consciously or unconsciously determines the frame of their thought. Because this is so one is justified in saying that even in the scientific view of reality an element of faith is effective. Scientists rightly try to prevent these elements of faith and philosophical truth from interfering with their actual research. This is possible to a great extent; but even the most protected experiment is not absolutely "pure"—pure in the sense of the exclusion of interfering factors such as the observer, and as the interest which determines the kind of question asked of nature in an experiment. What we said about the philosopher must also be said about the scientist. Even in his scientific work he is a human being, grasped by an ultimate concern, and he asks the question of the universe as such, the philosophical question.

In the same way the historian is consciously or unconsciously a philosopher. It is quite obvious that every task of the historian beyond the finding of facts is dependent on evaluations of historical factors, especially the nature of man, his freedom, his determination, his development out of nature, etc. It is less obvious but also true that even in the act of finding historical facts philosophical presuppositions are involved. This is especially true in deciding, out of the infinite number of happenings in every infinitely small moment of time, which facts shall be called historically relevant facts. The historian is further forced to give his evaluation of sources and their reliability, a task which is not independent of his interpretation of human nature. Finally, in the moment in which a historical work gives implicit or explicit assertions about the meaning of historical

events for human existence, the philosophical presuppositions of history are evident. Where there is
philosophy there is expression of an ultimate concern; there is an element of faith, however hidden it
may be by the passion of the historian for pure facts.

All these considerations show that, in spite of
their essential difference, there is an actual union of
philosophical truth and the truth of faith in every
philosophy and that this union is significant for the
work of the scientist and the historian. This union
has been called "philosophical faith."* The term is
misleading, because it seems to confuse the two elements, philosophical truth and the truth of faith.
Further, the term seems to indicate that there is *one*
philosophical faith, a "philosophia perennis," as it
has been termed. But only the philosophical question is perennial, not the answers. There is a continuous process of interpretation of philosophical
elements and elements of faith, not *one* philosophical faith.

There is truth of faith in philosophical truth.
And there is philosophical truth in the truth of faith.
In order to see the latter point we must confront the
conceptual expression of philosophical truth with
the symbolical expression of the truth of faith. Now,

---

*In the book of this name by Jaspers.

one can say that most philosophical concepts have mythological ancestors and that most mythological symbols have conceptual elements which can and must be developed as soon as the philosophical consciousness has appeared. In the idea of God the concepts of being, life, spirit, unity and diversity are implied. In the symbol of the creation concepts of finitude, anxiety, freedom and time are implied. The symbol of the "fall of Adam" implies a concept of man's essential nature, of his conflict with himself, of his estrangement from himself. Only because every religious symbol has conceptual potentialities is "theo-logy" possible. There is a philosophy implied in every symbol of faith. But faith does not determine the movement of the philosophical thought, just as philosophy does not determine the character of one's ultimate concern. Symbols of faith can open the eyes of the philosopher to qualities of the universe which otherwise would not have been recognized by him. But faith does not command a definite philosophy, although churches and theological movements have claimed and used Platonic, Aristotelian, Kantian or Humean philosophies. The philosophical implications of the symbols of faith can be developed in many ways, but the truth of faith and the truth of philosophy have no authority over each other.

5. THE TRUTH OF FAITH AND ITS CRITERIA

In what sense, then, can one speak of the truth of faith if it cannot be judged by any other kind of truth, whether scientific, historical or philosophical? The answer follows from the nature of faith as the state of being ultimately concerned. It has, as the concept of concern itself, two sides, a subjective and an objective side. The truth of faith must be considered from both sides. From the subjective side one must say that faith is true if it adequately expresses an ultimate concern. From the objective side one must say that faith is true if its content is the really ultimate. The first answer acknowledges the truth in all genuine symbols and types of faith. It justifies the history of religion and makes it understandable as a history of man's ultimate concern, of his response to the manifestation of the holy in many places in many ways. The second answer points to a criterion of ultimacy by which the history of religion is judged, not in terms of rejection but in terms of a yes and no.

Faith has truth in so far as it adequately expresses an ultimate concern. "Adequacy" of expression means the power of expressing an ultimate concern in such a way that it creates reply, action, communication. Symbols which are able to do this are alive. But the life of symbols is limited.

The relation of man to the ultimate undergoes changes. Contents of ultimate concern vanish or are replaced by others. A divine figure ceases to create reply, it ceases to be a common symbol and loses its power to move for action. Symbols which for a certain period, or in a certain place, expressed truth of faith for a certain group now only remind of the faith of the past. They have lost their truth, and it is an open question whether dead symbols can be revived. Probably not for those to whom they have died! If we look from this point of view at the history of faith, including our own period, the criterion of the truth of faith is whether or not it is alive. This, certainly, is not an exact criterion in any scientific sense, but it is a pragmatic one that can be applied rather easily to the past with its stream of obviously dead symbols. It cannot be applied so easily to the present because one never can say a symbol is definitely dead if it is still accepted. It may be dormant but capable of being reawakened.

The other criterion of the truth of a symbol of faith is that it expresses the ultimate which is really ultimate. In other words, that it is not idolatrous. In the light of this criterion the history of faith as a whole stands under judgment. The weakness of all faith is the ease with which it becomes idolatrous. The human mind, Calvin has said, is a continuously working factory of idols. This is true of all types of faith, and even if Protestant Christianity is considered as the point in which the different types converge, it is open to idolatrous distortions. It must also apply against itself the criterion which it uses against other forms of faith. Every type of faith has the tendency to elevate its concrete symbols to absolute validity. The criterion of the truth of faith, therefore, is that it implies an element of self-negation. That symbol is most adequate which expresses not only the ultimate but also its own lack of ultimacy. Christianity expresses itself in such a symbol in contrast to all other religions, namely, in the Cross of the Christ. Jesus could not have been the Christ without sacrificing himself as Jesus to himself as the Christ. Any acceptance of Jesus as the Christ which is not the acceptance of Jesus the crucified is a form of idolatry. The ultimate concern of the Christian is not Jesus, but the Christ Jesus who is manifest as the crucified. The event which has created this symbol has given the criterion by which the truth of Christianity, as well as of any other religion, must be judged. The only infallible truth of faith, the one in which the ultimate itself is unconditionally manifest, is that any truth of faith stands under a yes-or-no judgment.

Driven by this criterion, Protestantism has criticized the Roman Church. Doctrinal formulations did not divide the churches in the Reformation period; it was the rediscovery of the principle that no church has the right to put itself in the place of the ultimate. Its truth is judged by the ultimate. In the same way, Biblical research in Protestantism has shown the many levels of Biblical literature and the impossibility of considering the Bible as containing the infallible truth of faith. The same criterion is valid with respect to the whole history of religion and culture. The criterion contains a Yes—it does not reject any truth of faith in whatever form it may appear in the history of faith—and it contains a No—it does not accept any truth of faith as ultimate except the one that no man possesses it. The fact that this criterion is identical with the Protestant principle and has become reality in the Cross of the Christ constitutes the superiority of Protestant Christianity.

VI

⧉

THE LIFE OF FAITH

1. Faith and Courage

Everything said about faith in the previous chapters is derived from the experience of actual faith, of faith as a living reality, or in a metaphoric abbreviation, of the life of faith. This experience is the subject of our last chapter. The "dynamics of faith" are present not only in the inner tensions and conflicts of the content of faith, but also present in the life of faith, and of course the one is dependent on the other.

Where there is faith there is tension between participation and separation, between the faithful one and his ultimate concern. We have used the metaphor "being grasped" for describing the state of ultimate concern. And being grasped implies that he who is grasped and that by which he is grasped are, so to speak, at the same place. Without some participation in the object of one's ultimate concern, it is not possible to be concerned about it. In this sense every act of faith presupposes participation in that toward which it is directed. Without a preceding experience of the ultimate no faith in the ultimate can exist. The mystical type of faith has emphasized this point most strongly. Here lies its truth which no theology of "mere faith" can destroy. Without the manifestation of God in man the question of God and faith in God are not possible. There is no faith without participation!

But faith would cease to be faith without separation—the opposite element. He who has faith is separated from the object of his faith. Otherwise he would possess it. It would be a matter of immediate certainty and not of faith. The "in-spite-of element" of faith would be lacking. But the human situation, its finitude and estrangement, prevents man's participation in the ultimate without both the separation and the promise of faith. Here the limit of mysticism becomes visible: it neglects the human predicament and the separation of man from the ultimate. There is no faith without separation.

Out of the element of participation follows the certainty of faith; out of the element of separation follows the doubt in faith. And each is essential for the nature of faith. Sometimes certainty conquers doubt, but it cannot eliminate doubt. The conquered of today may become the conqueror of tomorrow. Sometimes doubt conquers faith, but it still contains faith. Otherwise it would be indifference. Neither faith nor doubt can be eliminated, though each of them can be reduced to a minimum, in the life of faith. Since the life of faith is life in the state of ultimate concern and no human being can exist completely without such a concern, we can say: Neither faith nor doubt can be eliminated from man as man.

Faith and doubt have been contrasted in such a way that the quiet certainty of faith has been praised as the complete removal of doubt. There is, indeed, a serenity of the life in faith beyond the disturbing struggles between faith and doubt. To attain such a state is a natural and justified desire of every human being. But even if it is attained—as in people who are called saints and in others who are described as firm in their faith—the element of doubt, though conquered, is not lacking. In the saints it appears, according to holy legend, as a temptation which increases in power with the increase of saintliness. In those who rest on their unshakable faith, pharisaism and fanaticism are the unmistakable symptoms of doubt which has been repressed. Doubt is overcome not by repression but by courage. Courage does not deny that there is doubt, but it takes the doubt into itself as an expression of its own finitude and affirms the content of an ultimate concern. Courage does not need the safety of an unquestionable conviction. It includes the risk without which no creative life is possible. For example, if the content of someone's ultimate concern is Jesus as the Christ, such faith is not a matter of a doubtless certainty, it is a matter of daring courage with the risk to fail. Even if the confession that Jesus is the Christ is expressed in a strong and positive way, the fact that it is a confession implies courage and risk.

All this is said of living faith, of faith as actual concern, and not of faith as a traditional attitude without tensions, without doubt and without courage. Faith in this sense, which is the attitude of many members of the churches as well as of society at large, is far removed from the dynamic character of faith as described in this book. One could say that such conventional faith is the dead remnant of former experiences of ultimate concern. It is dead but it can become alive. For even nondynamic faith lives in symbols. In these symbols the power of original faith is still embodied. Therefore, one should not underestimate the importance of faith as a traditional attitude. It is not actual, not living faith; it is potential faith which can become actual. This is especially relevant for education. It is not meaningless to communicate to children or immature adults objective symbols of faith and with them expressions of the living faith of former generations. The danger of this method, of course, is that the faith, mediated in education, will remain a traditional attitude and never break through to a state of living faith. However, if this causes people to become hesitant about communicating any of the given symbols and to wait until independent questions about the meaning of life have arisen, it can lead to a powerful life of faith, but it also can lead to emptiness, to cynicism and, in reaction to it, to idolatrous forms of ultimate concern.

Living faith includes the doubt about itself, the courage to take this doubt into itself, and the risk of courage. There is an element of immediate certainty in every faith, which is not subject to doubt, courage and risk—the unconditional concern itself. It is experienced in passion, anxiety, despair, ecstasy. But it is never experienced in isolation from a concrete content. It is experienced in, with and through the concrete content, and only the analytic mind can isolate it theoretically. Such theoretical isolation is the basis of this whole book; it is the way to the definition of faith as ultimate concern. But the life of faith itself does not include such analytic work. Therefore, the doubt about the concrete content of one's ultimate concern is directed against faith in its totality, and faith as a total act must affirm itself through courage.

The use of the term "courage" in this context (fully explained in my book *The Courage to Be*) needs some interpretation, especially in its relation to faith. In a short formulation one could say that courage is that element in faith which is related to the risk of faith. One cannot replace faith by courage, but neither can one describe faith without courage. In mystical literature the "vision of God" is described as the stage which transcends the state of faith either after the earthly life or in rare moments within it. In the complete reunion with the divine ground of being, the element of distance is overcome and with it uncertainty, doubt, courage and risk. The finite is taken into the infinite; it is not extinguished, but it is not separated either. This is not the ordinary human situation. To the state of separated finitude belong faith and the courage to risk. The risk of faith is the concrete content of one's ultimate concern. But it may not be the truly ultimate about which one is concerned. Religiously speaking, there may be an idolatrous element in one's faith. It may be one's own wishful thinking which determines the content; it may be the interest of one's social group which holds us in an obsolete tradition; it may be a piece of reality which is not sufficient to express man's ultimate concern, as in old and new polytheism; it may be an attempt to use the ultimate for one's own purposes, as in magic practices and prayers in all religions. It may be the confusion of the bearer of the ultimate with the ultimate itself. This is done in all types of faith and has been, from the first gospel stories on, the permanent danger of Christianity. A protest against such a confusion is found in the Fourth Gospel, which has Jesus say: "He who believes in me does not believe in me but in him who has sent me." But the classical dogma, the liturgies and the devotional life are not kept free from it. Nevertheless, the Christian can have the courage to affirm his faith in Jesus as the Christ. He is aware of the possibility and even the inevitability of idolatrous deviations, but also of the fact that in the picture of the Christ itself the criterion against its idolatrous abuse is given—the cross.

Out of this criterion comes the message which is the very heart of Christianity and makes possible the courage to affirm faith in the Christ, namely, that in spite of all forces of separation between God and man this is overcome from the side of God. One of these forces of separation is a doubt which tries to prevent the courage to affirm one's faith. In this situation faith still can be affirmed if the certainty is given that even the failure of the risk of faith cannot separate the concern of one's daring faith from the ultimate. This is the only absolute certainty of faith which corresponds with the only absolute content of faith, namely, that in relation to the ultimate we are always receiving and never giving. We are never able to bridge the infinite distance between the infinite and the finite from the side of the finite. This alone makes the courage of faith possible. The risk of failure, of error and of idolatrous distortion can be taken, because the failure cannot separate us from what is our ultimate concern.

2. Faith and the Integration of the Personality

The last consideration is decisive for the relation of faith to the problems of man's life as a personality. If faith is the state of being ultimately concerned, all preliminary concerns are subject to it. The ultimate concern gives depth, direction and unity to all other concerns and, with them, to the whole personality. A personal life which has these qualities is integrated, and the power of a personality's integration is his faith. It must be repeated at this point that such an assertion would be absurd if faith were what it is in its distorted meaning, the belief in things without evidence. Yet the assertion is not absurd, but evident, if faith is ultimate concern.

Ultimate concern is related to all sides of reality

and to all sides of the human personality. The ultimate is one object besides others, and the ground of all others. As the ultimate is the ground of everything that is, so ultimate concern is the integrating center of the personal life. Being without it is being without a center. Such a state, however, can only be approached but never fully reached, because a human being deprived completely of a center would cease to be a human being. For this reason one cannot admit that there is any man without an ultimate concern or without faith.

The center unites all elements of man's personal life, the bodily, the unconscious, the conscious, the spiritual ones. In the act of faith every nerve of man's body, every striving of man's soul, every function of man's spirit participates. But body, soul, spirit, are not three parts of man. They are dimensions of man's being, always within each other; for man is a unity and not composed of parts. Faith, therefore, is not a matter of the mind in isolation, or of the soul in contrast to mind and body, or of the body (in the sense of animal faith), but is the centered movement of the whole personality toward something of ultimate meaning and significance.

Ultimate concern is passionate concern; it is a matter of infinite passion. Passion is not real without a bodily basis, even if it is the most spiritual passion. In every act of genuine faith the body participates, because genuine faith is a passionate act. The way in which it participates is manifold. The body can participate both in vital ecstasy and in asceticism leading to spiritual ecstasy. But whether in vital fulfillment or vital restriction, the body participates in the life of faith. The same is true of the unconscious strivings, the so-called instincts of man's psyche. They determine the choice of symbols and types of faith. Therefore, every community of faith tries to shape the unconscious strivings of its members, especially of the new generations. If the faith of somebody expresses itself in symbols which are adequate to his unconscious strivings, these strivings cease to be chaotic. They do not need repression, because they have received "sublimation" and are united with the conscious activities of the person. Faith also directs man's conscious life by giving it a central object of "con-centration." The disrupting trends of man's consciousness are one of the great problems of all personal life. If a uniting center is absent, the infinite variety of the encountered world, as well as of the inner movements of the human mind, is able to produce or complete disintegration of the personality. There can be no other uniting center than the ultimate concern of the mind. There are various ways in which faith unites man's mental life and gives it a dominating center. It can be the way of discipline which regulates the daily life; it can be the way of meditation and contemplation; it can be the way of concentration on the ordinary work, or on a special aim or on another human being. In each case, faith is presupposed; none of it could be done without faith. Man's spiritual function, artistic creation, scientific knowledge, ethical formation and political organization are consciously or unconsciously expressions of an ultimate concern which gives passion and creative *eros* to them, making them inexhaustible in depth and united in aim.

We have shown how faith determines and unites all elements of the personal life, how and why it is its integrating power. In doing so we have painted a picture of what faith can do. But we have not brought into this picture the forces of disintegration and disease which prevent faith from creating a fully integrated personal life, even in those who represent the power of faith most conspicuously, the saints, the great mystics, the prophetic personalities. Man is integrated only fragmentarily and has elements of disintegration or disease in all dimensions of his being.

One can also say that the integrating power of faith has healing power. This statement, however, needs comment in view of linguistic and actual distortions of the relation of faith and healing. Linguistically (and materially) one must distinguish the integrating power of faith from what has been called "faith healing." Faith healing, as the term is actually used, is the attempt to heal others or oneself by mental concentration on the healing powers in others or in oneself. There is such healing power in nature and man, and it can be strengthened by mental acts. In a nondepreciating sense one could speak of the use of magic power; and certainly there is healing magic in human relationships as well as in the relation to oneself. It is a daily experience and sometimes one that is astonishing in its intensity and success. But one should not use the word "faith" for it, and one should not confuse it with the integrating power of an ultimate concern.

The integrating power of faith in a concrete situation is dependent on the subjective and objective factors. The subjective factor is the degree to which a person is open for the power of faith, and how strong and passionate is his ultimate concern. Such openness is what religion calls "grace." It is given and cannot be produced intentionally. The objective factor is the degree to which a faith has conquered its idolatrous elements and is directed toward the really ultimate. Idolatrous faith has a definite dynamic: it can be extremely passionate and exercise a preliminary integrating power. It can heal and unite the personality, including its soul and body. The gods of polytheism have shown healing power, not only in a magic way but also in terms of genuine reintegration. The objects of modern secular idolatry, such as nation and success, have shown healing power, not only by the magic fascination of a leader, a slogan or a promise but also by the fulfillment of otherwise unfulfilled strivings for a meaningful life. But the basis of the integration is too narrow. Idolatrous faith breaks down sooner or later and the disease is worse than before. The one limited element which has been elevated to ultimacy is attacked by other limited elements. The mind is split, even if each of these elements represents a high value. The fulfillment of the unconscious drives does not last; they are repressed or explode chaotically. The concentration of the mind vanishes because the object of concentration has lost its convincing character. Spiritual creativity shows an increasingly shallow and empty character, because no infinite meaning gives depth to it. The passion of faith is transformed into the suffering of unconquered doubt and despair, and in many cases into an escape to neurosis and psychosis. Idolatrous faith has more disintegrating power than indifference, just because it is faith and produces a transitory integration. This is the extreme danger of misguided, idolatrous faith, and the reason why the prophetic Spirit is above all the Spirit which fights against the idolatrous distortion of faith.

The healing power of faith raises the question

of its relation to other agencies of healing. We have already referred to an element of magic influence from mind to mind without referring to the medical art, its scientific presuppositions and its technical methods. There is an overlapping of all agencies of healing and none of them should claim exclusive validity. Nevertheless, it is possible conceptually to limit each of them to a special function. Perhaps one can say that the healing power of faith is related to the whole personality, independent of any special disease of body or mind, and effective positively or negatively in every moment of one's life. It precedes, accompanies and follows all other activities of healing. But it does not suffice alone in the development of the personality. In finitude and estrangement man is not a whole, but is disrupted into different elements. Each of these elements can disintegrate independently of the other elements. Parts of the body can become sick, without producing mental disease; and the mind can become sick without visible bodily failures. In some forms of mental sickness, especially neurosis, and in almost all forms of bodily disease the spiritual life can remain completely healthy and even gain in strength. Therefore, medical art must be used wherever such separated elements of the whole of the personality are disintegrating for external or internal reasons. This is true of mental as well as of bodily medicine. And there is no conflict between them and the healing power of the state of ultimate concern. It is also clear that medical activities, including mental healing, cannot produce a reintegration of the personality as a whole. Only faith can do this. The tension between the two agencies of health would disappear if both sides knew their special functions and their special limits. Then they would not be worried about the third agency, the healing by magic concentration on the powers of healing. They would accept its help while revealing at the same time its great limitations.

There are as many types of integrated personalities as there are types of faith. There is also the type of integration which unites many characteristics of the different types of personal integration. It was this kind of personality which was created by early Christianity, and missed again and again in the history of the Church. Its character cannot be described from the point of view of faith alone; it leads to the questions of faith and love, and of faith and action.

3. Faith, Love and Action

Since the apostle Paul was attacked because of his doctrine that faith in divine forgiveness and not human action makes man acceptable to God, the question of faith in relation to love and action has been asked and answered in many ways. The question and answer mean something quite different if faith is understood as the belief in things without evidence or if faith is understood as the state of being ultimately concerned. In the first case, it is natural to deny any direct dependence of love and action on faith; in the second case, love and action are implied in faith and cannot be separated from it. In spite of all distortions in the interpretation of faith, the latter is the classical doctrine however inadequately it was expressed.

One is ultimately concerned only about something to which one essentially belongs and from which one is existentially separated. There is no faith, we have seen, in the quiet vision of God. But there is infinite concern about the possibility of reaching such quiet vision. It presupposes the reunion of the separated; the drive toward the reunion of the separated is love. The concern of faith is identical with the desire of love: reunion with that to which one belongs and from which one is estranged. In the great commandment of the Old Testament, confirmed by Jesus, the object of ultimate concern, and the object of unconditional love, is God. From this is derived the love of what is God's, represented by both the neighbor and oneself. Therefore, it is the "fear of God" and the "love of Christ" which, in the whole Biblical literature, determines the behavior toward the other human beings. In Hinduism and Buddhism it is the faith in the ultimate One, from whom every being comes and to which it strives to return, that determines the participation in the other one. The consciousness of ultimate identity in the One makes identification with all beings possible and necessary. This is not the Biblical concept of love, which is person-centered, but it is love in the sense of the desire for reunion with that to which one belongs. In both types of faith, love and action are not commended as something external to faith (as it would be if faith were less than ultimate concern) but are elements of the concern itself. The separation of faith and love is always the consequence of a deterioration of religion. When Judaism became a system of ritual laws, when the Indian religions developed into a magic sacramentalism, when Christianity fell into both distortions and added doctrinal legalism, the question of the relation of faith to love became a stumbling block for people inside and outside these religions, and many turned away to nonreligious ethics.

They tried to escape distorted forms of faith by rejecting faith altogether. But the question is: is there such a thing as love without faith? There is certainly love without the acceptance of doctrines; history has shown that the most terrible crimes against love have been committed in the name of fanatically defended doctrines. Faith as a set of passionately accepted and defended doctrines does not produce acts of love. But faith as the state of being ultimately concerned implies love, namely, the desire and urge toward the reunion of the separated.

The question, however, remains whether or not love is possible without faith. Can a man love who has no ultimate concern? This is the right form of the question. The answer, of course, is that there is no human being without an ultimate concern and, in this sense, without faith. Love is present, even if hidden, in a human being; for every human being is longing for union with the content of his ultimate concern.

We have discussed distortions of the meaning of faith. It is equally necessary, though impossible in our limited framework, to reject misinterpretations of the meaning of love. One of them, however, must be mentioned: the reduction of love to an emotion. As in faith, emotion is connected with the experience of love. But this does not make love itself an emotion. Love is the power in the ground of everything that is, driving it beyond itself toward reunion with the other one and ultimately with the ground itself from which it is separated.

Different types of love have been distinguished, and the Greek *eros* type of love has been contrasted with the Christian *agape* type of love. *Eros* is described as the desire for self-fulfillment by the other being, *agape* as the will to self-surrender for the sake of the other being. But this alternative does not exist. The so-called "types of love" are actually "qualities of love," lying within each other and driven into conflict only in their distorted forms. No love is real without a unity of *eros* and *agape*. *Agape* without *eros* is obedience to a moral law, without warmth, without longing, without reunion. *Eros* without *agape* is chaotic desire, denying the validity of the claim of the other one to be acknowledged as an independent self, able to love and to be loved. Love as the unity of *eros* and *agape* is an implication of faith. The more love is implied the more faith has conquered its demonic-idolatrous possibilities. An idolatrous faith which gives ultimacy to a preliminary concern stands against all other preliminary concerns and excludes love relations between the representatives of contrasting claims. The fanatic cannot love that against which his fanaticism is directed. And idolatrous faith is by necessity fanatical. It must repress the doubts which characterize the elevation of something preliminary to ultimacy.

The immediate expression of love is action. Theologians have discussed the question of how faith can result in action. The answer is: because it implies love and because the expression of love is action. The mediating link between faith and works is love. When the Reformers, who believed salvation to be dependent on faith alone, criticized the Roman Catholic doctrine that works are necessary for salvation they were right in denying that any human action can produce reunion with God. Only God can reunite the estranged with himself. But the Reformers did not realize, and the Catholics were still only dimly aware of it, that love is an element of faith if faith is understood as ultimate concern. Faith implies love, love lives in works: in this sense faith is actual in works. Where there is ultimate concern there is the passionate desire to actualize the content of one's concern. "Concern" in its very definition includes the desire for action. The kind of action is, of course, dependent on the type of faith. Faith of the ontological type drives toward elevation above the separation of being from being. Faith of the ethical type drives toward transformation of the estranged reality. In both of them love is working. In the first case, the *eros* quality of loves drives to union with the beloved in that which is beyond the lover and the beloved. In the second case, the *agape* quality of love drives to acceptance of the beloved and his transformation into what he potentially is. Mystical love unites by negation of the self. Ethical love transforms by affirmation of the self. The sphere of activities following from mystical love is predominantly ascetic. The sphere of activities following from ethical love is predominantly formative. In both cases, faith determines the kind of love and the kind of action.

These are examples describing a basic polarity in the character of faith. There are many other possible examples. Lutheran faith in personal forgiveness is less conducive to social action than the Calvinistic faith in the honor of God. The humanist faith in the essential rationality of man is more favorable for general education and democracy than the traditionally Christian faith in original sin and the demonic structures of reality. The Protestant faith, in an unmediated, person-to-person encounter with God, produces more independent personalities than the Catholic faith and its ecclesiastical mediation between God and man. Faith as the state of being ultimately concerned implies love and determines action. It is the ultimate power behind both of them.

4. THE COMMUNITY OF FAITH AND ITS EXPRESSIONS

In our description of the nature of faith we have shown that faith is real only in the community of faith, or more precisely, in the communion of a language of faith. The consideration of love and faith has pointed in the same direction: love is an implication of faith, namely, the desire toward reunion of the separated. This makes faith a matter of community. Finally, since faith leads to action and action presupposes community, the state of ultimate concern is actual only within a community of action.

The problems arising from this situation with respect to faith and doubt have been discussed. But the creedal expressions to which this discussion referred are of secondary importance, and there are more fundamental expressions of the ultimate concern in a community of faith. As we have seen before, all expressions of ultimate concern are symbolic, because the ultimate cannot be expressed in nonsymbolic terms. But one must distinguish two basic forms of symbolic expression—the intuitive and the active; in traditional terms—the mythical and the ritual. The community of faith constitutes itself through ritual symbol and interprets itself in mythical symbols. The two are interdependent: what is practiced in the cult is imagined in the myth, and conversely. There is no faith without these two ways of self-expression. Even if nation or success is the content of faith, rites and myths are connected with them. It is well known that totalitarian systems have an elaborated system of ritual activities, and that they have a grasp of imaginative symbols, which, however absurd they may be, express the faith underlying the whole system. The totalitarian community expresses itself in ritual activities and intuitive symbols in a way that has many similarities to the ways an authoritarian religious group expresses itself. However, in all genuine religions there is a protest against the idolatrous elements which are accepted without restriction by political totalitarianism.

The life of faith is life in the community of faith, not only in its communal activities and institutions but also in the inner life of its members. Separation from the activities of the community of faith is not necessarily separation from the community itself. It can be a way (for example, in voluntary seclusion) to intensify the spirit which rules the communal life. Often he who has withdrawn into temporary seclusion returns to the community whose language he still speaks and whose symbols he renews. For there is no life of faith, even in mystical solitude, which is not life in the community of faith. Further, there is no community where there is not a community of faith. There are groups bound together by a mutual interest, favoring a unity as long as the interest lasts. There are groups which have grown up naturally as families and tribes, and will die a natural death when the conditions of their life disappear. Neither of these two groups in itself is a community of faith. Whether a group comes into existence in the natural way or in the way of common interest, it is a transitory group. It must come to an end when the technical or biological conditions of its existence vanish. In a community of faith these conditions are not decisive; the only condition of its continuation is the vitality of its faith. That which is based on an ultimate concern is not exposed to destruction by preliminary concerns and the lack of their fulfillment. The most astonishing proof of this assertion is the history of the Jews. They are, in the history of mankind, the document of the ultimate and unconditional character of faith.

Neither the cultural nor the mythological expressions of faith are meaningful if their symbolic character is not understood. We have tried to show the distorting consequences of literalism, and it often happens that in opposition to literalism, myth and cult are attacked as such and almost removed from a community of faith. The myth is replaced by a philosophy of religion, the cult is replaced by a code of moral demands. It is possible for such a state to last for a while because the original faith is still effective in it. Even the negation of the expressions of faith does not negate the faith itself—at least not in the beginning. This is the reason one can point to a nonreligious morality of a high order and can attempt to deny the interdependence of faith and morals. But there is a limit to this possibility. Without an ultimate concern as its basis every system of morals degenerates into a method of adjustment to social demands, whether they are ultimately justified or not. And the infinite passion which characterizes a genuine faith evaporates and is replaced by a clever calculation which is unable to withstand the passionate attacks of an idolatrous faith. This is a description of what has happened on a large scale in Western civilization. It is concealed only by the fact that in many representatives of humanist faith, moral strength was and is greater than in members of a religiously active community. But this is a transitory stage. There is still faith in these men, ultimate concern about human dignity and personal fulfillment. There is religious substance in them, which, however, can be wasted in the next generation if the faith is not renewed. This is possible only in the community of faith under the continuous impact of its mythical and cultic symbols.

One of the reasons why independent morals are turned against their religious roots is the distorted meaning which symbol and myth have received in the history of religion, including the history of the Christian churches. The ritual symbols of faith have been distorted into magic realities which are effective like physical forces, even if they are not accepted in an act of faith as expressions of one's ultimate concern. They are loaded with a sacred power which works if man does not resist its working. This super-

stitious interpretation of the sacramental act arouses
the protest of the humanists and drives them toward
the ideal of morals without religion. The rejection
of sacramental superstition was one of the main
points in the Protestant protest. But historical Protestantism removed through its protest not only cultic superstition but also the genuine meaning of
ritual, and of the sacramental symbols. In this way
Protestantism, against its will, has supported the
trend toward independent morals. But faith cannot
remain alive without expressions of faith and the
personal participation in them. This insight has
driven Protestantism to a new evaluation of cult and
sacrament in our period. Without symbols in which
the holy is experienced as present, the experience of
the holy vanishes.

The same is true of the mythological expression
of one's ultimate concern. If the myth is understood
literally, philosophy must reject it as absurd. It must
demythologize the sacred stories, transform the
myth into a philosophy of religion and finally into a
philosophy without religion. But the myth, if interpreted as the symbolic expression of ultimate concern, is the fundamental creation of every religious
community. It cannot be replaced by philosophy or
by an independent code of morals.

Cult and myth keep faith alive. No one is completely without them; for no one is completely with-

out an ultimate concern. Few understand their meaning and their power, although the life of faith is dependent on them. They express the faith of a community and produce personal faith in the members of the community. Without them, without the community in which they are used, faith would disappear and man's ultimate concerns would go into hiding. Then would come the short hour of independent morals.

5. The Encounter of Faith with Faith

There are many communities of faith, not only in the religious realm but also in secular culture. In our present world most of them are in mutual contact and show predominantly an attitude of tolerance toward each other. But there are some important exceptions; it may well be that more of them will develop under the political and social pressures of our period. Exceptions are above all the secular-political types of faith. These include not only the totalitarian ones but, in reaction to them and in defense of themselves, the democratic ones also. There are also exceptions in the religious realm: the official doctrine of the Roman Church concerning its exclusive possession of the truth; the negative way in which Protestant fundamentalism looks at all other forms of Christianity and religion. Intolerance as a characteristic of faith can easily be understood. If faith is the state of being ultimately concerned, and if every ultimate concern must express itself concretely, the special symbol of the ultimate concern participates in its ultimacy. It participates in its unconditional character, although it is not unconditional itself. This situation which is the source of idolatry is also the source of intolerance. The one expression of the ultimate denies all other expressions. It becomes—almost inevitably—idolatrous and demonic. This has happened to all religions which take the concrete expression of their ultimate concern seriously. It also has happened to Christianity, although the symbol of the Cross stands against the self-elevation of a concrete religion to ultimacy, including Christianity. The advantage of classical mysticism is that it does not take the concrete expression of one's ultimate concern seriously and, therefore, can trespass the set of concrete symbols on which every religion is based. Such an indifference to the concrete expression of the ultimate is tolerant, but it lacks the power to transform the existential distortions of reality. In Judaism and Christianity reality is transformed in the name of the God of history. The exclusive monotheism of the prophets, the struggle against the limited gods of paganism, the message of universal justice in the Old and of universal grace in the New Testatment—all this made Judaism, Islam and Christianity intolerant of any kind of idolatry. These religions of justice, history and the expectation of the end could not accept the mystical tolerance of India. They are intolerant and can become fanatical and idolatrous. This is the difference between the exclusive monotheism of the prophets and the transcendent monotheism of the mystics.

The question is: Must the encounter of faith with faith lead either to a tolerance without criteria or to an intolerance without self-criticism? If faith is understood as the state of being ultimately concerned, this alternative is overcome. The criterion of every faith is the ultimacy of the ultimate which it tries to express. The self-criticism of every faith is the insight into the relative validity of the concrete symbols in which it appears.

From this the meaning of conversion can be understood. The term "conversion" has connotations which make its use difficult. It can mean the awakening from a state in which an ultimate concern is lacking (or more exactly, hiddden) to an open and conscious awareness of it. If conversion means this, every spiritual experience is an experience of conversion.

Conversion also can mean the change from one set of beliefs to another. Conversion in this sense is of no ultimate concern. It might or it might not happen. It is important only if, in the new belief, the ultimacy of the ultimate concern is better preserved than in the old belief. If this is the case, conversion is of great importance.

A most important case of an encounter of faith with faith in the Western world is the encounter of Christianity with forms of secular belief. For secularism is never without an ultimate concern; therefore, the encounter with it is an encounter of faith with faith. In such an encounter two ways of action are adequate to the situation and two are not. The two ways adequate to the situation are, first, the methodological inquiry into those elements of the conflict which can be approached by inquiry and, second, the witness to those elements of the conflict which drive to conversion. The combination of these two ways is the adequate attitude in the encounter of faith with faith. It acknowledges that an ultimate concern is not a matter of arguments and admits that in the expressions of an ultimate concern there are elements which are subject to discussion on the pure cognitive level. In every struggle about the symbols of faith this double way must be used. This would dissolve fanaticism about the concrete expression of faith and confirm the ultimate concern as a matter of a total personal participation. Conversion is not a matter of prevailing arguments, but it is a matter of personal surrender.

The argumentative side lies on another level. If missions try to bring about the conversion of many from one faith to another, they try to bring about the unity of faith in humanity as a whole. Nobody can be certain that such unity will be reached in the course of human history; nobody can deny that such unity is the desire and hope of mankind in all periods and in all places. But there is no way of reaching this unity except by distinguishing ultimacy itself from that in which ultimacy expresses itself. The way to a universal faith is the old way of the prophets, the way of calling idolatry idolatry and rejecting it for the sake of that which is really ultimate. Such faith may never be able to express itself in *one* concrete symbol, although it is the hope of every great religion that it will provide the all-embracing symbol in which the faith of man universally will express itself. Such a hope is only justified if a religion remains aware of the conditional and non-ultimate character of its own symbols. Christianity expresses this awareness in the symbol of the "cross of the Christ"—even if the Christian churches neglect the meaning of this symbol by attributing ultimacy to their own particular expression of ultimacy. The radical self-criticism of Christianity makes it most capable of universality—so long as it maintains this self-criticism as a power in its own life.

Conclusion: The Possibility and Necessity of Faith Today

Faith is real in every period of history. This fact does not prove that it is an essential possibility and necessity. It could be—like superstition—an actual distortion of man's true nature. This is what many people who reject faith believe. The question raised by this book is whether such belief is based on insight or on misunderstanding, and the answer is unambiguously that the rejection of faith is rooted in a complete misunderstanding of the nature of faith. Many forms of this misunderstanding, many misrepresentations and distortions of faith have been discussed. Faith is a concept—and a reality—which is difficult to grasp and to describe. Almost every word by which faith has been described—also on the preceding pages—is open to new misinterpretations. This cannot be otherwise, since faith is not a phenomenon beside others, but the central phenomenon in man's personal life, manifest and hidden at the same time. It is religious and transcends religion, it is universal and concrete, it is infinitely variable and always the same. Faith is an essential possibility of man, and therefore its existence is necessary and universal. It is possible and necessary also in our period. If faith is understood as what it centrally is, ultimate concern, it cannot be undercut by modern science or any kind of philosophy. And it cannot be discredited by its superstitions or authoritarian distortions within and outside churches, sects and movements. Faith stands upon itself and justifies itself against those who attack it, because they can attack it only in the name of another faith. It is the triumph of the dynamics of faith that any denial of faith is itself an expression of faith, of an ultimate concern.

Marion Pauck

Paul Tillich was one of the great theologian/philosophers of the twentieth century. Born in Germany, he studied at the universities of Halle and Tübingen, and was an army chaplain in the First World War. After the war, he taught briefly at the University of Berlin and the University of Frankfurt. Dismissed by Hitler's Nazi government in 1933, he was invited to teach at Union Theological Seminary in New York, where he stayed for twenty-two years. He became a University Professor at Harvard and delivered the Gifford Lectures. Author of fourteen books, as well as the three-volume *Systematic Theology* and three volumes of sermons, he was a prolific author, a mesmerizing teacher, and a charismatic preacher.